REGENTS RESTORATION DRAMA SERIES

General Editor: John Loftis

THE RIVAL QUEENS

NATHANIEL LEE

The Rival Queens

Edited by

P. F. VERNON

UNIVERSITY OF NEBRASKA PRESS · LINCOLN

Copyright © 1970 by the University of Nebraska Press
All Rights Reserved
Standard Book Number: 8032–0375–6
Library of Congress Catalog Card Number: 72–91330

MANUFACTURED IN THE UNITED STATES OF AMERICA

Regents Restoration Drama Series

The Regents Restoration Drama Series provides soundly edited texts, in modern spelling, of the more significant plays of the late seventeenth and early eighteenth centuries. The word "Restoration" is here used ambiguously and must be explained. If to the historian it refers to the period between 1660 and 1685 (or 1688), it has long been used by the student of drama in default of a more precise word to refer to plays belonging to the dramatic tradition established in the 1660's, weakening after 1700, and displaced in the 1730's. It is in this extended sense—imprecise though justified by academic custom— that the word is used in this series, which includes plays first produced between 1660 and 1737. Although these limiting dates are determined by political events, the return of Charles II (and the removal of prohibitions against operation of theaters) and the passage of Walpole's Stage Licensing Act, they enclose a period of dramatic history having a coherence of its own in the establishment, development, and disintegration of a tradition.

Some twenty editions having appeared as this volume goes to press, the series has reached nearly a half of its anticipated range of between forty and fifty volumes. The volumes will continue to be published for a number of years, at the rate of three or more annually. From the beginning the editors have planned the series with attention to the projected dimensions of the completed whole, a representative collection of Restoration drama providing a record of artistic achievement and providing also a record of the deepest concerns of three generations of Englishmen. And thus it contains deservedly famous plays—*The Country Wife*, *The Man of Mode*, and *The Way of the World*— and also significant but little known plays, *The Virtuoso*, for example, and *City Politiques*, the former a satirical review of scientific investigation in the early years of the Royal Society, the latter an equally satirical review of politics at the time of the Popish Plot. If the volumes of famous plays finally achieve the larger circulation, the other volumes may conceivably have the greater utility, in making available texts otherwise difficult of access with the editorial apparatus needed to make them intelligible.

The editors have had the instructive example of the parallel and senior project, the Regents Renaissance Drama Series; they have in fact used the editorial policies developed for the earlier plays as their own, modifying them as appropriate for the later period and as the experience of successive editions suggested. The introductions to the separate Restoration plays differ considerably in their nature. Although a uniform body of relevant information is presented in each of them, no attempt has been made to impose a pattern of interpretation. Emphasis in the introductions has necessarily varied with the nature of the plays and inevitably—we think desirably—with the special interests and aptitudes of the different editors.

Each text in the series is based on a fresh collation of the seventeenth- and eighteenth-century editions that might be presumed to have authority. The textual notes, which appear above the rule at the bottom of each page, record all substantive departures from the edition used as the copy-text. Variant substantive readings among contemporary editions are listed there as well. Editions later than the eighteenth century are referred to in the textual notes only when an emendation originating in some one of them is received into the text. Variants of accidentals (spelling, punctuation, capitalization) are not recorded in the notes. Contracted forms of characters' names are silently expanded in speech prefixes and stage directions and, in the case of speech prefixes, are regularized. Additions to the stage directions of the copy-text are enclosed in brackets.

Spelling has been modernized along consciously conservative lines, but within the limits of a modernized text the linguistic quality of the original has been carefully preserved. Contracted preterites have regularly been expanded. Punctuation has been brought into accord with modern practices. The objective has been to achieve a balance between the pointing of the old editions and a system of punctuation which, without overloading the text with exclamation marks, semicolons, and dashes, will make the often loosely flowing verse and prose of the original syntactically intelligible to the modern reader. Dashes are regularly used only to indicate interrupted speeches, or shifts of address within a single speech.

Explanatory notes, chiefly concerned with glossing obsolete words and phrases, are printed below the textual notes at the bottom of each page. References to stage directions in the notes follow the admirable system of the Revels editions, whereby stage directions are keyed, decimally, to the line of the text before or after which they occur.

Thus, a note on 0.2 has reference to the second line of the stage direction at the beginning of the scene in question. A note on 115.1 has reference to the first line of the stage direction following line 115 of the text of the relevant scene. Speech prefixes, and any stage directions attached to them, are keyed to the first line of accompanying dialogue.

JOHN LOFTIS

June, 1969
Stanford University

Contents

List of Abbreviations

C1	Collected works, 1713
C2	Collected works, 1722
C3	Collected works, 1734
M-J	Dougald MacMillan and Howard Mumford Jones, eds. *Plays of the Restoration and Eighteenth Century.* New York, 1931.
OED	*Oxford English Dictionary*
om.	omitted
Q1	First quarto, 1677
Q2	Second quarto, 1684
Q3	Third quarto, 1690
Q4	Fourth quarto, 1694
Q7	Seventh quarto, 1702
S-C	Thomas B. Stroup and Arthur L. Cooke, eds. *The Works of Nathaniel Lee.* New Brunswick, N.J., 1954, 1955.
S.D.	stage direction
S.P.	speech prefix

Introduction

The Rival Queens, or the Death of Alexander the Great, the fourth and most popular of Lee's plays, was published in 1677; the first edition (Q1), a carefully printed quarto, was recorded in *The Term Catalogues* for Michaelmas Term (November) of that year.[1] A second quarto (Q2) of 1684, the year in which Lee was committed to Bedlam, attempts to regularize the idiosyncratic punctuation of Q1, corrects a few obvious errors, and introduces a number of unsatisfactory variants. The last edition to appear during Lee's lifetime (Q3) is a quarto of 1690, which follows Q2 closely. There are two quartos dated 1694: the first (Q4) was printed for "R. Bentley," the other was set line-by-line from Q4, but has the spelling "Bently" in the imprint, and is probably a pirated edition of somewhat later date.[2] Further quartos appeared in 1699, 1702 (Q7), and 1704. Excluding the piracy from the series, each of the quartos after Q2 follows that immediately preceding page-by-page with few substantive variants. The play was included in three early eighteenth-century collections of Lee's works. C1 (1713) introduces many new errors; C2 (1722) corrects several of these and makes sensible emendations, but without returning to the earlier quartos; C3 (1734) follows C2 closely. *The Rival Queens* was reprinted separately on nearly thirty more occasions during the eighteenth and nineteenth centuries, and it was included in many collections of British drama.[3] The drastically revised version of the text used on the late eighteenth-century stage was first published in 1770; J. P. Kemble's adaptation, printed in 1796, includes further revisions. In this century the play has appeared only twice: in *Plays of the Restoration and Eighteenth Century,* edited by D. MacMillan and H. M. Jones (1931), and in the collected edition of Lee's *Works,* edited by T. B. Stroup and A. L. Cooke (1954, 1955).

[1] Edward Arber, ed., *The Term Catalogues* (London, 1903–1906), I, 291.

[2] See Fredson Bowers, "Nathaniel Lee: Three Probable Seventeenth-Century Piracies," *Papers of the Bibliographical Society of America,* XLIV (1950), 62–66.

[3] C. J. Stratman, *A Bibliography of English Printed Tragedy 1565–1900* (Carbondale and Edwardsville, Ill., 1966), pp. 346–349.

The present modernized edition uses as copy-text the British Museum copy of Q1, and is based on a collation of Q1–3. In cases of special interest substantive variants from later editions have been recorded in the textual notes.

The stage-history of *The Rival Queens* is extraordinary and deserves special consideration.[4] The first performance took place before royalty on March 17, 1677, at the Theatre Royal in Dury Lane.[5] The cast was led by Charles Hart, a celebrated Othello and Brutus, and the creator of leading rôles in many of Dryden's plays. Hart's performances, no doubt based on the author's own accomplished recitation of the text, apparently emphasized the royal bearing and grace of Alexander.[6] Statira was played by Elizabeth Boutell, a petite actress with a voice described as "weak, tho' very mellow," and an air of childlike innocence which had made her a natural choice for the part of Wycherley's country wife two years before.[7] The original Roxana was Rebecca Marshall, an actress well practiced in the interpretation of imperious and fiery characters. Records of only nine further performances in the seventeenth century have survived, but the play was evidently outstandingly successful; Colley Cibber, who thought little of it, noted, with some irritation, that "there was no one Tragedy, for many Years, more in favour with the Town."[8] When Hart died, only six years after the first performance, the part of Alexander was taken over by Cardell Goodman, a notorious gamester and adventurer, and by William Mountfort, who seems to have

[4] For a number of references concerning the stage-history of the play I am indebted to Nancy Eloise Lewis, "Nathaniel Lee's *The Rival Queens*: A Study of Dramatic Taste and Technique in the Restoration" (Ph.D. dissertation, Ohio State University, 1957). Details of seventeenth- and eighteenth-century performances are given in *The London Stage*, ed. William Van Lennep and others (Carbondale, Illinois, 1960–).

[5] Warrant for payment of £10 for performance before royalty on March 17, dated June 1, 1677, P.R.O., L.C. 5/141, p. 359 (quoted in A. Nicoll, *A History of English Drama 1660–1900* [Cambridge, 1952], I, 345–346). This is confirmed as the first performance by a letter from the Marquis of Worcester dated March 17, 1676/7, H.M.C. 12th Report, Appendix, Beaufort MSS, ix, 66 (quoted in *The London Stage*, I, 255).

[6] John Downes, *Roscius Anglicanus*, ed. Montague Summers (London, [1928]), p. 16. Mohun's praise of Lee's impassioned reading of his own work at rehearsal is recorded by Colley Cibber, *An Apology for the Life of Mr. Colley Cibber* (London, 1740), p. 68.

[7] *The History of the English Stage*, "By Mr. Thomas Betterton," generally attributed to E. Curll (London, 1741), p. 21.

[8] Cibber, *Apology*, p. 64.

offered an attractively tender and passionate interpretation.[9] The play was given a new lease of life when, late in his career, Thomas Betterton, the greatest actor of the age, undertook the rôle, probably along lines close to Hart's original performances.[10] Mrs. Marshall was succeeded in the part of Roxana by Elizabeth Barry, whose expressive range has been vividly recorded by a contemporary observer. He was especially impressed by her handling of Roxana's second speech (III.45–57):

> I have heard this Speech spoken in a Rage that run the Actor out of Breath; but Mrs. *Barry* when she talked of her *hot bleeding Heart*, seemed to feel a Fever within, which by *Debate* and *Reason* she would *quench*. This was not done in a ranting Air, but as if she were strugling with her Passions, and trying to get the Mastery of them; a peculiar *Smile* she had, which made her look the most genteely malicious Person that can be imagined.[11]

The partnership of Mrs. Barry and Anne Bracegirdle, who assumed the rôle of Statira, contributed indirectly to the dramatic influence of *The Rival Queens*. Lee's pattern of contrasted female characters had soon become part of the stock-in-trade of tragic dramatists, and the two actresses were repeatedly called upon to represent the spectacle of innocent virtue persecuted by raging vice. Their popularity in such parts encouraged still more dramatists to adopt the convention.[12]

For the first seventy-five years of the eighteenth century the astonishing total of almost two hundred performances spread over fifty different seasons is recorded.[13] At first the musical elements were expanded: Italian singers were employed and elaborate dances introduced. Then, in 1756, a revised version was adopted. Billed as *Alexander the Great*, the title which had long replaced the original in common usage, this omits the ghost and singing spirits, shortens a number of other passages, turns what remains of the encounter between the rival queens into blank verse, simplifies and rearranges Lee's language throughout, and offers "The Triumphal Entry of

[9] Ibid., p. 76.
[10] See Thomas Davies, *Dramatic Miscellanies* (London, 1784), III, 271–272.
[11] *History of the English Stage*, pp. 19–20.
[12] On the dramatic importance of these two actresses, see Eric Rothstein, *Restoration Tragedy: Form and the Process of Change* (Madison, Wisconsin, 1967), pp. 141–144.
[13] See *The London Stage*.

Alexander into Babylon" as a grand, spectacular attraction. The actor J. P. Kemble introduced more alterations in 1795, giving further opportunity for scenic display, including "Bucephalus, Amazons, elephants, cars, bridges, battles, banquets, and processions."[14] The play remained on the stock-lists of the English and American theaters until well into the second half of the nineteenth century.[15]

The enthusiastic response of the original audiences is reflected in three other plays which were given their first performances during the same year.[16] John Banks based much of *The Rival Kings* on identical sections of the French romance that Lee had drawn on for his plot. The list of characters attached to Samuel Pordage's *The Siege of Babylon* corresponds closely to that of *The Rival Queens*. Dryden, who later, in *Alexander's Feast* (1697), chose the conqueror's varying moods to illustrate the expressive powers of music, openly acknowledged his admiration for Lee's tragedy by providing commendatory verses for the first edition, and the powerful effect it had on him is evident in *All for Love*. The rivalry of Octavia and Cleopatra, their bitter meeting in the third act, and the characterization of the blunt, but loyal, general Ventidius, must have reminded the first audience strongly of the earlier play, since the parts of Antony, Ventidius, and Cleopatra were taken by the very same players who had created Alexander, Clytus, and Statira. Although Dryden had previously announced his dissatisfaction with rhymed dialogue, Lee's successful example probably confirmed him in his decision to experiment with blank verse.

Within a short period *The Rival Queens* attained the status of a popular, but somewhat antiquated, classic. Arousing a curious blend of reluctant admiration, affection, condescension, and amusement, it became part of the familiar language of the theater. The first allusions to it are respectful enough. William Mountfort, for example, the actor previously mentioned, brought into his farcical adaptation of Marlowe's *Doctor Faustus* (1688) the spirits of "the Famous *Alexander* fighting with his great Rival *Darius* in their true Shapes, and State

[14] D. E. Baker, *Biographia Dramatica* (London, 1812), III, 211.

[15] For a summary of American performances, see Thomas B. Stroup and Arthur L. Cooke, eds., *The Works of Nathaniel Lee* (New Brunswick, N.J., 1954, 1955), I, 213, 467.

[16] My discussion of the play's influence and of Lee's treatment of his sources is considerably indebted to William Van Lennep, "The Life and Works of Nathaniel Lee ... A Study of Sources" (Ph.D. dissertation, Harvard University, 1933), pp. 138–191.

Majestical."[17] But by the 1690's most references are humorous. Thus the impudent hero of Farquhar's *The Constant Couple*, mocking a woman who rejects his advances, insists that she must have "just come flush from reading the *Rival Queen*," and launches into Alexander's part.[18] In *Natural Magic* (1697), a brief farce by Peter Motteux, one character jumps on another's back, shouting, in imitation of the mad Alexander, "See, see how fast the brave Dutch Squadrons gallop. *Bear me*, Bucephalus, *among the Billows!*"[19] Comic dramatists even quote isolated lines from the play without indicating the source. When Cynthia, in Congreve's *The Double-Dealer*, tells her father of her vow never to marry any man other than Mellefont, the audience must have instantly recognized the familiar reply: "But did you swear, did that sweet Creature swear!"[20] Thomas D'Urfey uses Alexander's "Spite, by the gods, proud spite, and burning envy!" (IV.ii.143) in a similar context.[21] Statira's "Then he will talk, good gods, how he will talk" (I.ii.48), twisted and absurdly applied, became part of the intimate banter of well-educated men throughout the eighteenth century.[22] "When Greeks joined Greeks" (IV.ii.138) became, with frequent misquotation, the proverbial phrase "when Greek meets Greek."

The tragedy was also burlesqued on more than one occasion. In *The Rival Queans*, by Colley Cibber, first performed over thirty years after the original, the women's parts were taken by men, and Lee's poetic technique ridiculed line by line. A burlesque opera, *The Court of Alexander*, by George Alexander Stevens, which makes many comic allusions to *The Rival Queens*, was performed in 1770. During the second half of the eighteenth century there were at least four more burlesques;[23] another, by Thomas Dibdin, was performed as late as 1837.[24]

[17] *The Life and Death of Doctor Faustus* (London, 1697), p. 20.

[18] *The Complete Works of George Farquhar*, ed. Charles Stonehill (London, 1930), I, 141.

[19] *The Novelty: Every Act a Play* (London, 1697), p. 49. Cf. *The Rival Queens*, V.ii.15.

[20] *The Complete Plays of William Congreve*, ed. Herbert Davis (Chicago, 1967), p. 171. Cf. *The Rival Queens*, II.350.

[21] *The Intrigues at Versailles* (London, 1697), p. 11.

[22] Before Addison singled out this line in *Spectator* 39 (April 14, 1711), John Dennis had already quoted it in *A Plot and No Plot* (London, 1697), p. 33.

[23] See Nicoll, *History of English Drama*, III, 271, 318; Baker, *Biographia Dramatica*, II, 14.

[24] See Van Lennep, "Nathaniel Lee," p. 669.

Early critical comments on the play display a similar ambivalence. On the credit side one comes across repeated references to the fire and vigor which Dryden praises in his introductory verses, and to the moving qualities of the tragedy. But Lee's ability to control the intense passion he brings to his theme was frequently questioned; his subsequent madness seemed to confirm the image of a writer who allowed a lively imagination to range beyond the bounds of reason and judgment. His use of hyperbole and grandiose imagery gave particular offense and was commonly condemned as rant, fustian, or bombast.

To account for the mixed feelings evoked by the play, it is necessary to consider *The Rival Queens* in the light of changes which were taking place in the form of serious drama at the time when it was written.[25] The Restoration heroic play, despite the masterly theoretical support provided by its leading practitioner, Dryden, had encountered resistance from the start, and proved to be little more than a short-lived novelty on the stage. The aim of this type of drama was to arouse admiration for its noble heroes and heroines: the leading characters, placed in difficult military and romantic situations, made impeccable decisions which might stand as a pattern for the audience. It followed naturally from this didactic purpose that the model heroes and heroines should be seen to succeed. A highly ornamented verse form was considered appropriate, since the actions were performed by men and women of superior mold, and the heroic couplet was found to be particularly well adapted to the generalized level of moral argument from which the characters arrived at their decisions. The attractions of heroic drama soon palled, however, and by the mid-1670's a number of dramatists, including Lee, were beginning to introduce features which would quickly undermine the heroic form from within and oust it from the stage. The aim of the pathetic tragedy, which replaced it, was to enlarge the humane feelings of the audience by engaging its sympathy for the leading characters in their sufferings. Although the perfect and successful hero may merit admiration, he invites little sympathy or pity; so the characterization of the hero and the fortunate ending had to be altered. An audience is likely to sympathize most with characters in familiar situations; tragic dramatists, therefore, tended to shift from public to private issues, even though they continued to write about figures of national importance. As

25 My remarks on the changing form of serious drama are heavily indebted to the excellent discussion in Rothstein, *Restoration Tragedy.*

women were particularly vulnerable, and liable to suffer extreme personal distress, they occupied a more central position in pathetic tragedy. The heroic couplet became redundant, since a verse form was needed which could represent passion and suffering with some immediacy.

The Rival Queens was among those plays which contributed to the change in serious drama. Belonging wholly to neither form, it is more varied and less predictable than most late seventeenth-century tragedies. Yet its links with a dying genre rapidly became a liability; original when it first appeared, it soon grew outmoded. The heroic strain is discernible in the conception of the main character. A great conqueror and a passionate lover, he tries to live at a superhuman level; and the courtier who is reported to have said of Hart's Alexander that he "might Teach any King on Earth how to Comport himself" evidently felt that the character was meant to embody a heroic lesson.[26] Those passages which concern the love of Lysimachus for Parisatis are typical of heroic drama: the audience is invited to admire the faithfulness and courage of Lysimachus and to rejoice in the just union of the lovers. Lee even reverts to heroic couplets in the debate between the rival queens, and he outdoes Dryden in the language of high-flown boasts and threats. What really disturbed the eighteenth-century critics was Lee's retention of these once fashionable features, which had since become ridiculous. Precisely the same objections would have been leveled at the heroic plays of Dryden and Boyle, had they survived. As it happened, apart from Lee's own *Theodosius*, *The Rival Queens* was the only example of the genre regularly available to later audiences. Its survival was due in part to Lee's anticipation of later tragic patterns. The central figure is at best a hero in decline, and his glorious reputation only serves to intensify our pity as we watch his disintegration and the misery he unwittingly inflicts on a totally innocent woman. Lee's use of blank verse is only one of a number of steps in the evolution of a poetic style capable of representing the quickly changing emotions of all three leading characters.

In *The Rival Queens*, however, pathos is not, as it is in so many of the tragedies that followed it, an end in itself. Emotional participation is made to serve a theme of far-reaching contemporary significance: the limits of authority. Lee's thoughtful and coherent interpretation of Alexander's career stresses not, as might be expected, the conqueror's

[26] Downes, *Roscius Anglicanus*, p. 16.

great military victories, but the king's failure to recognize the independent rights of his subjects. It is not difficult to see why this aspect
of Alexander's rule should have attracted the dramatist's attention.
By insisting upon an equally inflexible view of monarchy, the last
English king had reduced the country to a state of civil war, and both
his sons were soon to discover that the problem of determining the
limits of the royal prerogative had not yet been settled. This is not
necessarily to imply that, when Lee wrote the play, he was consciously
thinking in terms of the English political situation. The Popish Plot
scandal, which provided a convenient rallying-point for the various
opposition forces, and drove men to take up clearly defined positions,
was still more than a year off, and it is quite possible that Lee had not
yet come to any firm political conclusions. The play contains relatively few generalizations, which suggests that Lee may simply have
responded favorably to the passages criticizing Alexander's despotism
in his classical sources, Plutarch's *Life* and the *History of Alexander* by
Quintus Curtius, without realizing their full implications. On the
other hand, his first play, *Nero*, had revealed an early interest in the
subject of arbitrary rule;[27] and only three and a half years later *Lucius
Junius Brutus* was to be banned from the stage for its transparent use
of a classical theme to expound a theory of government which favored
limitations on the monarchy.[28] It could even be argued that the
meeting of Alexander's rival queens was intended to recall the occasion when Charles II introduced his mistress, Lady Castlemaine, to
Queen Catherine. The scene in which Alexander tries to force Clytus
to wear Persian dress could hardly have failed to remind a Restoration
audience of the stir created by their own king when, earlier in his
reign, he had introduced into his court the new fashion of the Persian
"vest."[29] These specific parallels may be no more than accidental, and
Lee himself may not have regarded *The Rival Queens* as a political
play, but his interpretation of the classical story is certainly strongly
colored by controversial ideas arising out of the most grave political
issue of the century.

His selection and arrangement of the historical material draws

[27] The political overtones of Lee's early plays are discussed in F. Barbour,
"The Unconventional Heroic Plays of Nathaniel Lee," *Studies in English,
University of Texas* (1940), 109–116.

[28] See introduction to *Lucius Junius Brutus*, ed. John Loftis (Lincoln, Nebr.,
1967), pp. xii–xix.

[29] These possible topical allusions were suggested to me by Mr. C. P.
Vernier, who is currently preparing a dissertation on "Politics and the
London Stage in the Reign of Charles II" at University College, London.

attention to the worst features of Alexander's rule. By postponing the murder of Clytus, which in fact took place long before Alexander's death, he was able to represent the intense resentment felt by the Macedonian veterans when their leader began to adopt the customs of a nation they had conquered, and to emulate the luxury and arbitrary power of the Persian despots. Since Clytus is introduced as a man of tact and patience, concerned to prevent the outbreak of disorder, the dramatization of his outspoken protest leads to the conclusion that, although the assassination plot may be the work of ambitious malcontents, Alexander's behavior has driven even well-disposed loyalists to breaking-point. Allusions scattered throughout the play add up to a fearsome charge-sheet, which includes almost all the cruel and wanton attempts to crush resistance, real or imaginary, which marred Alexander's expedition. Lee seldom allows the audience to forget one historical fact, to which he obviously attached the greatest significance: Alexander's claim to be of divine descent.

At first sight, the fictional material, which Lee found in La Calprenède's prose romance, *Cassandre*, appears to have little bearing on the subject of Alexander's qualities as a ruler.[30] But on closer examination Lee's treatment of the romantic incidents can be seen to have raised social issues which may well have seemed relevant at the time. Alexander's two marriages are mentioned in both the historical sources and in *Cassandre*, but the events of the French story take place after the king's death, and there the two women compete for the hand of a quite different, unmarried lover. By making Alexander the object of their rivalry, Lee has created the curious situation of a love story which concerns bigamy. Instead of dealing with it as such, however, he has translated the alien custom into terms with which a Restoration audience would have been familiar. For, although Roxana is referred to as Alexander's first wife, little mention is made of her marriage rights; it is only Alexander's infidelity towards Statira that is considered a serious breach of solemn vows. Statira, in fact, is presented as a true, virtuous wife; Roxana, lustful, ambitious, and spiteful, is given all the characteristics conventionally associated with the cast-off mistress. Alexander himself speaks of his return to Statira after the fashion of a monogamous husband repenting a relapse into his former libertinism. His behavior towards her is thus closely related to a type of arrogance criticized in other Restoration plays, deriving from a male-orientated view of marriage, which assumes that

[30] Lee used the translation by Sir Charles Cotterell, first published, as *Cassandra*, in 1652.

a wife should dutifully forgive her husband's sexual lapses as soon as he has offered a suitable show of remorse. Statira, on the other hand, treats marriage as a contract: when her husband breaks his side of the bargain, the contract becomes void, and she is entitled to a separation. Lysimachus, by disobeying Alexander, is asserting the right of the individual members of a family to choose their own partners in marriage regardless of the wishes of its head. In arranging the marriage of his sister-in-law to a man she does not want, Alexander insists upon an authoritarian view of family relationships which was being openly questioned at this time, in literature, if not in real life. A parallel between the authority of kings, of husbands, and of family heads may now appear far-fetched, but it was a fundamental premise in the political thought of the late seventeenth century. Theoretical controversy over the divine right of kings hinged on the rights of a husband and father over his wife and family. The very title of Sir Robert Filmer's famous exposition of divine right, *Patriarcha*,[31] indicates its central assumption; while, conversely, Locke, the leading advocate of constitutional monarchy, was concerned to establish the natural independence of the mature child and the contractual nature of marriage. In contemporary terms Lee's interpretation of Alexander's practice in political and domestic government was all of a piece.

The dramatist's own position is expressed indirectly through various forms of irony. The most striking examples concern the king's boasted divinity. The flattering words which greet him on his first entrance, "O son of Jupiter, live forever" (II.96), follow hard on preparations for his assassination, and contrast pathetically with the contemptuous realism of Cassander's comments on "this mortal god that soon must bleed" (II.72). The arrogant toast, "Live all, you must: 'tis a god gives you life" (IV.ii.71) is spoken at the very moment when Alexander raises the poisoned cup which is to put an end to his own life. One of the most tense moments in the play occurs when Clytus, who has already exasperated the king by continual talk of his earthly father, Philip, turns on the story of the oracle with devastating sarcasm:

> Why should I fear to speak a truth more noble
> Than e'er your father Jupiter Ammon told you:
> Philip fought men, but Alexander women.
>
> (IV.ii.140–142)

[31] Published posthumously in 1680, though written before 1642.

The king's obsessive concern to assert his authority is treated with similar irony. "My word," he declares, "Like destiny, admits not a reverse" (II.387–388); yet in the course of the action his word is seldom obeyed. His first command of any importance is instantly refused by Lysimachus; his hopes of a happy reunion with Statira are quickly shattered by the announcement of her independent decision; and even Clytus, the soldier, is eventually driven to disobey orders. Roxana never takes the slightest notice of his instructions, unless they happen to suit her convenience, and simply ignores his impotent outbursts in their last scene together. Lee was certainly a little careless about his stage-directions, but it can surely be no accident that when, towards the end of the play, Alexander issues frantic orders for the crucifixion of an innocent man, the tearing of clothes, and the destruction of buildings, there are no indications that the actors were expected to make the least movement.

As G. Wilson Knight has pointed out in a perceptive discussion of the play, Lee demonstrates with some subtlety the effects of tyranny on the tyrant himself.[32] Alexander's lack of self-awareness and his self-imposed blindness to truths which are obvious to those around him would be almost comic, were it not for his noble stature and his intense personal suffering. "Contain yourself, dread sir" (II.266)—Clytus's words come at the very moment when Alexander is congratulating himself on his tolerance and self-control. Again and again Lee draws attention to the king's pathological need to hear his greatness confirmed by others, and his refusal to allow anyone else to voice an independent opinion. His frantic cry of victory at a time of total defeat is not merely the arbitrary effect of poison; alcohol and poison seem only to hasten a steady process of withdrawal into a world remote from reality. Those who knew Lee's tragedy could hardly have been shocked by Swift's choice of Alexander, in *A Tale of a Tub*, to represent the self-absorbed insanity which underlies political ambition.

In Lee's hands the stage picture is often given an almost symbolic function: the birds of prey fighting before the conspirators assemble; the conspirators dispersing as the triumphal march enters; Roxana, knife in hand, bursting into the bower of beauty, where the innocent Statira lies dreaming.[33] But the use of visual metaphor in the Act IV

[32] *The Golden Labyrinth* (London, 1962), pp. 160–163.
[33] The staging of Statira's murder owes much to Act V, scene iii, of Otway's *Alcibiades* (1675). The portents, the arrival of Alexander, and the

banquet scene to reinforce the ironies inherent in the dramatic situation is exceptionally imaginative. Cassander, standing alone on the stage, has just concluded his satanic soliloquy when the shutters open to reveal the grand, group tableau of Alexander on his throne, surrounded by his generals, caught at the height of his triumphant celebrations. Almost at once the splendor of the luxurious costumes is tarnished with the appearance of Lysimachus in his blood-stained shirt. Contrasted with the plain military dress and bearing of Clytus, the exotic dances seem to represent mere dissipation. His courageous independence is vividly impressed upon the audience in visual terms when he alone remains standing, while all the rest on stage fall down before Alexander. The king's attempt to win the affection of his men is turned into a pathetic charade by his ostentatious descent from the throne to sit upon the floor.

William Archer, in a damaging attack on the structure of *The Rival Queens*, complained that the play falls apart because Lee failed to provide any causal connection between the various episodes.[34] But once it is accepted that the main action is the fall of Alexander, and not, as Archer thought, the contest between the rival queens, his objection loses force. The first act establishes the four parallel forms of discontent which threaten to disturb Alexander's position of authority; each has arisen from, or has been aggravated by, the king's own actions. The way in which these various "broils" develop into direct rebellion, and their impact on the king, occupy the remaining acts. As one difficulty is settled, either permanently or temporarily, another rises in its place, with increasingly disastrous consequences. The delayed appearance of the main character is a device repeated on a smaller scale throughout the play, and calculated to produce both tension and dramatic irony. The audience, forewarned, is kept in a constant state of anxious anticipation; the hero, isolated in his ignorance, remains vulnerable to ever more disturbing emotional shocks. It is true that the conspiracy, being secret, can have no effect on Alexander until the end of the play, but Lee introduces it in the first scene and keeps it alive to provide suspense, so that the dénouement does not appear arbitrary. On the other hand, the conflict

---

interruption of the soothsayer show the influence of *Julius Caesar*, which had been performed by the King's Company only three months before.

[34] *The Old Drama and the New* (London, 1923), pp. 153–157.

between Statira and Roxana, both because their meeting is centrally placed, and because the extreme emotions of the two characters are portrayed in vivid detail, does make a greater dramatic impact than is strictly justified by its contribution to the plot. Its structural function is simply to divert the consequences of Alexander's faithlessness, to give him the illusion that the problem has been solved, when, in reality, Statira's voluntary separation from him has merely been exchanged for her death. The clash between the masculine and feminine personalities of the two women certainly creates tension, while Lee's presentation of Roxana's sadistic imagination shows insight, and even wit; but the confrontation tends to distract our attention from the main issues of the play. It does, however, help to make Alexander a more attractive protagonist; and this is important. The audience is meant to pity the king in his distress, and, were it not for the passionate expressions of both women, there would be little in the text, as distinct from the person and bearing of the actor, to make him at all sympathetic. The weakness of the Lysimachus-Parisatis episodes is not that they are irrelevant, but that they are banal. The conventional reunion of the lovers, in particular, works against the logic of the play, which demands the death of Lysimachus along with that of Clytus, Statira, and the many others who have challenged Alexander's authority in the past.

Lee's style in this play raises more awkward problems. Dryden identified the main characteristic of its rant when he wrote that all "was tempestuous and blustering; heaven and earth were coming together at every word."[35] Much of the imagery in *The Rival Queens* is, indeed, confined to the cosmic (world, sun, moon, stars), the elemental (fire, lightning, whirlwind), and the superhuman (fortune, destiny, heaven). In justice to Lee, it should be pointed out that he generally employed rant when he wished to imply criticism of the speaker. Dryden himself had put bombast to ironic use in the presentation of his tyrannic villains, and in the mouth of Alexander such images sound appropriate enough. He is, after all, meant to appear vainglorious; he does, absurdly, claim to be a god; and other characters remind us on more than one occasion that he is a splendid talker, whose actions by no means correspond to his words. Cassander and

[35] "A Parallel betwixt Poetry and Painting" (1695), in *Of Dramatic Poesy and Other Critical Essays*, ed. George Watson (London, 1962), II, 198.

Roxana, who indulge in similar verbal extravagances, are, likewise, excessively ambitious characters. But Lee does also seem to have imagined that his use of grand images would create awe and raise the particular situation to a more universal level. If he reckoned that a fashionable convention, which had already come under heavy fire, would continue to impress audiences in future generations, he made a sad miscalculation. Fortunately, for more passionate effects, he adopted a different style, which remained acceptable over a far longer period. This depends less on imagery than on rhetorical devices, such as breaking up the metrical line, and introducing oaths, exclamations, sighs, and other direct expressions of feeling. One convention he particularly favored was the repetition of a single word in a context that would allow the actor to vary the emotional intensity of each utterance, as in "O, turn thee, turn! Thou barb'rous brightness, turn!" (III.390). A rhetorical style of this kind relies heavily both on the audience's acceptance of relatively unstable conventions and on the availability of actors capable of using them expressively. Lee's methods lasted well; but by the middle of the eighteenth century the tragedy had to be wholly rewritten in a style which then seemed more effective. A hundred years later even the introduction of visual substitutes for the now dead rhetoric of both the original and the revised versions failed to arouse sufficient response.

Acting conventions have since changed so radically that the range of gestures and of vocal inflexions, for which Lee's text provides, now lies quite outside the compass to which modern actors and audiences are accustomed, though good performances of opera can still offer some idea of the kind of effect intended. Fortunately, a few theatergoers in the past tried to preserve something of their experience, and their accounts help us to imagine Mrs. Barry, as Roxana, following Alexander on her knees, and pleading "in so Pathetic a Manner, as drew Tears from the greatest Part of the Audience,"[36] or Spranger Barry, the leading interpreter of the revised version, whose

> address to his favourite queen was soft and elegant, and his love ardently passionate; in the scene with Clytus, in his rage, he was terrible; and, in his penitence and remorse, excessive. In his last distracting agony, his delirious laugh was wild and frantic, and his dying groan affecting.[37]

36 *History of the English Stage*, p. 22.
37 Davies, *Dramatic Miscellanies*, p. 277.

To dismiss such testimony as mere theatrical history, irrelevant to dramatic criticism, is to misunderstand the nature not only of *The Rival Queens* but of at least two centuries of English drama.

P. F. VERNON

King's College, London

THE RIVAL QUEENS

. . . Natura sublimis et acer,
Nam spirat tragicum satis, et feliciter audet.

... being gifted with spirit and vigor; for he has some tragic inspiration, and he is happy in his ventures (Horace *Epistles* II. i. 165–166; tr. H. Rushton Fairclough [Loeb Library]).

To the Right Honorable John, Earl of Mulgrave, Gentleman of His Majesty's Bedchamber, and Knight of the Most Noble Order of the Garter

MY LORD,

When I hear by many persons, not indifferent judges, how poets are censured most, even where they most intend to please, and sometimes, by those to whom they address, condemned for flatterers, sycophants, little fawning   5
wretches, I confess of all undertakings there is none more dreadful to me than a dedication. So nicely cruel are our judges, that, after a play has been generally applauded on the stage, the industrious malice of some after observers shall damn it for an epistle or a preface. For this reason,   10
my lord, Alexander was more to seek for a patron in my troubled thoughts than for the temple of Jupiter Ammon in the spreading wilds and rolling sands. 'Tis certain too he must have been lost, had not fortune, whom I must once at least acknowledge kind in my life, presented me to your   15
lordship. You were pleased, my lord, to read it over act by act, and by particular praises, proceeding from the sweetness, rather than the justice, of your temper, lifted me up from my natural melancholy and diffidence to a bold belief that what so great an understanding warranted could not   20
fail of success. And here I were most ungrateful, if I should not satisfy the judging world of the surprise I was in. Pardon me, my lord, for calling it a surprise, when I was first honored by waiting upon your lordship. So much unexpected and, indeed, unusual affability from persons of your birth and   25
quality, so true an easiness, such frankness, without affectation, I never saw. Your constant but few friends

23. it] *Q1; om. Q2–3.*   26. frankness,] *Q1;* frankness *Q2–3.*

Earl of Mulgrave] John Sheffield, third Earl of Mulgrave, afterwards Duke of Buckingham and Normanby (1648–1721), statesman, minor poet, and patron of Dryden.

12. *temple*] Alexander visited this famous oracle in the Libyan desert in 331 B.C., and was there greeted by the priests as the son of Jupiter Ammon.

12. *Ammon*] Egyptian god, later identified with Jupiter.

–3–

show the firmness of your mind, which never varies; so
godlike a virtue that a prince puts off his majesty when
he parts with resolution. In all the happy times that I   30
attended you, unless business or accident interposed, I
have observed your company to be the same. You have
traveled through all tempers, sailed through all humors
of the court's unconstant sea; you have gained the gallant
prizes which you sought, your selected, unvaluable friends;   35
and I am perfectly persuaded, if you traffic but seldom
abroad, 'tis for fear of splitting upon knaves or fools. Nor is
it pride, but rather a delicacy of your soul, that makes you
shun the sordid part of the world, the lees and dregs of it,
while in the noblest retirement you enjoy the finer spirits,   40
and have that just greatness to be above the baser. How
commendable therefore is such reservation; how admirable such a solitude! If you are singular in this, we ought
to blame the wild, unthinking, dissolute age: an age whose
business is senseless riot, Neronian gambols, and ridiculous   45
debauchery; an age that can produce few persons, beside
your lordship, who dare be alone. All our hot hours burnt
in night-revels, or drowned in day-dead-sleep; or if we
wake, 'tis a point of reeling honor jogs us to the field, where,
if we live or die, we are not concerned, for the soul was laid   50
out before we went abroad, and our bodies were after acted
by mere animal spirits without reason. When I more
narrowly contemplate your person, methinks I see in your
lordship two of the most famous characters that ever ancient
or modern story could produce: the mighty Scipio and the   55

46. beside] *Q1;* besides *Q2-3.*

---

35. *unvaluable*] invaluable.

45. *Neronian gambols*] Lee had dramatized this subject in his first play, *Nero* (1674).

50-51. *laid out*] i.e., like a corpse before burial.

51. *acted*] animated.

52. *animal spirits*] "the supposed 'spirit' or principle of sensation and voluntary motion" (*OED*).

55. *story*] history.

55. *Scipio*] Scipio Africanus, Roman general who defeated the Cartha-ginians at the end of the third century B.C. Lee had made him a leading character in his second play, *Sophonisba* (1675).

retired Cowley. You have certainly the gravity, temperance,
and judgment, as well as the courage, of the first; all which,
in your early attempts of war, gave the noblest dawn of
virtue, and will, when occasion presents, answer our
expectation and shine forth at full. Then, for the latter,   60
you possess all his sweetness of humor in peace, all that
halcyon tranquillity of mind, where your deep thoughts
glide, like silent waters, without a wrinkle, your hours move
with softest wings, and rarely any larum strikes to discom-
pose you. You have the philosophy of the first, and, which,   65
I confess, of all your qualities I love most, the poetry of the
latter. I was never more moved at Virgil's *Dido* than at a
short poem of your lordship's, where nothing but the
shortness can be disliked. As our churchmen wish there
were more noblemen of their function, so wish I, in the   70
behalf of depressed poetry, that there were more poets of
your lordship's excellence and eminence. If poetry be a
virtue, she is a ragged one, and never in any age went
barer than now. It may be objected, she never deserved less.
To that I must not answer; but I am sure when she merited   75
most, she was always dissatisfied, or she would not have forsaken the most splendid courts in the world. Virgil and
Horace, favorites of the mightiest emperor, retired from
him, preferring a mistress, or a white boy, and two or three
cheerful drinking friends in a country village to all the   80
magnificence of Rome. Or if sometimes they were snatched
from their cooler pleasures to an imperial banquet, we may

---

70. noblemen] noble-men *Q4;*
noble men *Q 1–3.*

---

56. *retired Cowley*] Abraham Cowley (1618–1667), poet and dramatist. He
retired to country estates outside London in 1663, and his *Several Discourses
by Way of Essays, in Verse and Prose* (published posthumously in 1668) is
chiefly concerned with the Horatian theme of rural retreat.

58. *your . . . war*] Mulgrave served as a volunteer against the Dutch in
the fleet commanded by Prince Rupert and the Duke of Albemarle in 1666.
He received command of a ship in 1673.

62. *halcyon*] calm; the halycon was a mythical bird, supposed to nest on
the sea, where it calmed the winds and waves.

64. *larum*] alarm, call to arms.

67. *Dido*] i.e., Book IV of the *Aeneid.*

79. *white*] fair.

see by their verses in praise of the country life 'twas against
their inclination: witness Horace in his Epode "*Beatus ille qui
procul*, etc.," part of his sixth Satire, his Epistle to Fuscus   85
Aristius, Virgil's Georgic "*O fortunatos nimium bona si*, etc.,"
all rendered by Mr. Cowley so copiously and naturally as
no age gone before, or coming after, shall equal, though all
heads joined together to outdo him. I speak not of his
exactness to a line, but of the whole. This then may be said   90
as to the condition of poets in all times: few ever arrived
to a middle fortune; most have lived at the lowest; none
ever mounted to the highest, neither by birth, for none was
ever born a prince, as no prince, to my remembrance, was
ever born a poet, nor by industry, because they were   95
always too much transported by their own thoughts from
minding the grave business of a world not of their humor.
Whereas even slaves, the rubbish of the earth, have, by
most prodigious fortune, gained a scepter, and with their
vile heads sullied the glories of a crown. Praise is the   100
greatest encouragement we chameleons can pretend to, or
rather the manna that keeps soul and body together; we
devour it as if it were angels' food, and vainly think we
grow immortal. For my own part, I acknowledge I never
received a better satisfaction from the applause of an   105
audience than I have from your single judgment. You gaze

83. the] *Q1*; a *Q2–3*.

---

84. *Epode*] *Epodes* II, 1–4: *Beatus ille qui procul negotiis,/ ut prisca gens mortalium,/ paterna rura bobus exercet suis/ solutus omni faenore.* Translated by Cowley: "Happy the Man whom bounteous Gods allow/ With his own Hands Paternal Grounds to Plough!/ Like the first golden Mortals Happy he/ From Business and the cares of Money free" (*Essays, Plays and Sundry Verses* ed. A. R. Waller [Cambridge, 1906], p. 412).

85. *Satire*] *Satires* I. vi.
85. *Epistle*] *Epistles* I. x.
86. *Georgic*] *Georgics* II. 458–460: *O fortunatos nimium, sua si bona norint,/ agricolas! quibus ipsa, procul discordibus armis,/ fundit humo facilem victum iustissima tellus.* Translated by Cowley: "Oh happy, (if his Happiness he knows)/ The Country Swain, on whom kind Heavn' bestows/ At home all Riches that wise Nature needs;/ Whom the just Earth with easie plenty feeds" (*Essays, Plays and Sundry Verses*, p. 409).
87. *all . . . Cowley*] in *Several Discourses*.
101. *chameleons*] believed to feed on air.
101. *pretend to*] aim at.

at beauties and wink at blemishes; and do both so gracefully that the first discovers the acuteness of your judgment, the other the excellency of your nature. And I can affirm to your lordship, there is nothing transports a poet, next to 110 love, like commending in the right place. Therefore, my lord, this play must be yours; and Alexander, whom I have raised from the dead, comes to you with an assurance answerable to his character and your virtue. You cannot expect him in his majesty of two thousand years ago. I have 115 only put his illustrious ashes in an urn, which are now offered, with all observance, to your lordship, by,

My lord,

Your lordship's most humble, obliged,

and devoted servant, 120

NAT. LEE

---

108. *discovers*] displays.

To Mr. Lee, on his *Alexander*

The blast of common censure could I fear,
Before your play my name should not appear;
For 'twill be thought, and with some color too,
I pay the bribe I first received from you,
That mutual vouchers for our fame we stand,   5
To play the game into each other's hand,
And as cheap penn'orths to ourselves afford
As Bessus and the brothers of the sword.
Such libels private men may well endure,
When states and kings themselves are not secure.   10
For ill men, conscious of their inward guilt,
Think the best actions on by-ends are built.
And yet my silence had not 'scaped their spite;
Then envy had not suffered me to write.
For since I could not ignorance pretend,   15
Such worth I must or envy or commend.
So many candidates there stand for wit,
A place in court is scarce so hard to get.
In vain they crowd each other at the door,
For ev'n reversions are all begged before.   20

---

3. *color*] superficial appearance of reason.

4. *bribe . . . you*] Earlier in the same year commendatory verses by Lee had been included in the first edition of *The State of Innocence*, Dryden's dramatic version of *Paradise Lost*.

7–8.] In Beaumont and Fletcher's *A King and No King* (1611), Bessus, a braggart soldier, declares: "They talk of fame: I have gotten it in the wars and will afford any man a reasonable pennyworth. Some will say . . . that it is to be achieved with danger; but my opinion is otherwise" (III.ii.1–4; ed. Robert K. Turner, Jr. [Lincoln, Nebr., 1963]). In Act IV, scene iii, he talks with extravagant courtesy to two "gentlemen o'th'sword," who address one another as "brother" and convince Bessus that to be thrashed is a mark of courage. *Penn'orth* (*pennyworth*) means both "small quantity" and "price for value, bargain"; *afford* means "give."

11. *ill*] evil.

12. *by-ends*] underhand, selfish purposes.

14. *Then . . . write*] i.e., then they would have said that envy prevented me from writing.

18. *place*] official employment in the service of the crown.

20. *reversions*] A *reversion* is "the right of succession to an office or place, after the death or retirement of the holder" (*OED*).

Desert, how known soe'er, is long delayed;
And then, too, fools and knaves are better paid.
Yet, as some actions bear so great a name
That courts themselves are just, for fear of shame,
So has the mighty merit of your play   25
Extorted praise, and forced itself a way.
'Tis here, as 'tis at sea; who farthest goes,
Or dares the most, makes all the rest his foes;
Yet when some virtue much outgrows the rest,
It shoots too fast and high to be oppressed;   30
As his heroic worth struck envy dumb,
Who took the Dutchman and who cut the boom.
Such praise is yours, while you the passions move,
That 'tis no longer feigned, 'tis real love,
Where nature triumphs over wretched art;   35
We only warm the head, but you the heart.
Always you warm! And if the rising year,
As in hot regions, bring the sun too near,
'Tis but to make your fragrant spices blow,
Which in our colder climates will not grow.   40
They only think you animate your theme
With too much fire, who are themselves all phlegm.
Prizes would be for lags of slowest pace,
Were cripples made the judges of the race.
Despise those drones, who praise while they accuse   45
The too much vigor of your youthful muse.
That humble style which they their virtue make
Is in your power; you need but stoop and take.
Your beauteous images must be allowed
By all but some vile poets of the crowd;   50
But how should any signpost-dauber know

30. oppressed] opprest *Q1;* exprest   46. your] *Q1;* you *Q2–3.*
Q2–3.

30. *oppressed*] trampled down.
32. *Who . . . boom*] Sir Edward Spragge (d. 1673), admiral. In 1671 he
destroyed a pirate fleet from Algiers in the Bay of Bugia, after cutting through
the boom which protected it. He took part in a number of actions against
the Dutch; cf. Dryden's *Annus Mirabilis,* l. 693.
42. *phlegm*] one of the four bodily humors in ancient physiology, a pre-
dominance of which led to coldness or indolence.
43. *lags*] the last in a race.

The worth of Titian or of Angelo?
Hard features every bungler can command;
To draw true beauty shows a master's hand.

JOHN DRYDEN   55

---

52. *Angelo*] Michelangelo.

PROLOGUE TO *ALEXANDER*

Written by Sir Car Scroope, Baronet

How hard the fate is of that scribbling drudge
Who writes to all, when yet so few can judge!
Wit, like religion, once divine was thought,
And the dull crowd believed as they were taught.
Now each fanatic fool presumes t'explain   5
The text, and does the sacred writ profane.
For, while you wits each other's fall pursue,
The fops usurp the power belongs to you.
You think y'are challenged in each new playbill,
And here you come for trial of your skill,   10
Where, fencer-like, you one another hurt,
While with your wounds you make the rabble sport.
Others there are that have the brutal will
To murder a poor play, but want the skill.
They love to fight, but seldom have the wit   15
To spy the place where they may thrust and hit;
And therefore, like some bully of the town,
Ne'er stand to draw, but knock the poet down.
With these like hogs in gardens it succeeds,
They root up all, and know not flowers from weeds.   20
As for you, sparks, that hither come each day
To act your own and not to mind our play,
Rehearse your usual follies to the pit,
And with loud nonsense drown the stage's wit;
Talk of your clothes, your last debauches tell,   25
And witty bargains to each other sell;

Car Scroope] Char. Scroop *Q1–3*.   4. believed] *Q2–3;* believed, *Q1.*
1. that] *Q1;* the *Q2–3.*

Sir Car Scroope] minor poet and courtier (1649–1680). He also wrote the
prologue to Etherege's *The Man of Mode* (1676) and a song for Lee's next
play, *Mithridates* (1678).

5. *fanatic*] afflicted with religious mania; a term often applied to religious
dissenters.

8. *fops*] fools.

18. *stand*] wait.

19. *succeeds*] happens.

26. *bargains . . . sell*] catch one another out with coarse jokes.

Gloat on the silly she, who for your sake
Can vanity and noise for love mistake,
Till the coquette, sung in the next lampoon,
Is by her jealous friends sent out of town.   30
For, in this duelling, intriguing age, ⎫
The love you make is like the war you wage; ⎬
Y'are still prevented ere you come t'engage. ⎭
But 'tis not to such trifling foes as you
The mighty Alexander deigns to sue.   35
You Persians of the pit he does despise,
But to the men of sense for aid he flies;
On their experienced arms he now depends,
Nor fears he odds, if they but prove his friends.
For as he once a little handful chose,   40
The numerous armies of the world t'oppose,
So, backed by you, who understand the rules,
He hopes to rout the mighty host of fools.

---

30. *jealous*] vigilant, apprehensive.
33. *still*] always.
42. *rules*] principles of good dramatic writing.

DRAMATIS PERSONAE

Men

ALEXANDER THE GREAT	Mr. Hart	
CLYTUS, master of his horse	Mr. Mohun	
LYSIMACHUS, prince of the blood	Mr. Griffin	
HEPHESTION, Alexander's favorite	Mr. Clarke	5
CASSANDER, son of Antipater ⎫	⎧ Mr. Kynaston	
POLYPERCHON, commander ⎪ conspirators	⎨	
of the phalanx ⎬	Mr. Goodman	
PHILIP, brother to Cassander ⎭	⎩ Mr. Powell	
THESSALUS, the Median	Mr. Wiltshire	10
PERDICCAS ⎫	⎧ Mr. Lydall	
EUMENES ⎬ great commanders	⎨ Mr. Watson	
MELEAGER ⎭	⎩ Mr. Perin	
ARISTANDER, a soothsayer	Mr. Coysh	
[SPIRIT OF DARIUS, late king of Persia]		15

Women

SYSIGAMBIS, mother of the royal family	Mrs. Corey	
STATIRA, daughter of Darius, married to		
Alexander	Mrs. Boutell	
ROXANA, daughter of Cohortanus, first		20
wife of Alexander	Mrs. Marshall	
PARISATIS, sister to Statira, in love with		
Lysimachus	Mrs. Baker	
[SPIRIT OF QUEEN STATIRA, mother of Statira]		
ATTENDANTS, SLAVES, GHOST, DANCERS, GUARDS[, PRIESTS,		25
PHYSICIANS]		

Scene: *Babylon*

6. Kynaston] Kenaston *Q 1–3.*

---

4. *of the blood*] of the royal family.

6. *Antipater*] regent in Macedonia during Alexander's Asian expedition.

8. *phalanx*] apparently used loosely for "infantry."

9. *Mr. Powell*] Martin Powell, father of the better known actor and dramatist, George Powell.

17. *mother*] i.e., mother of Darius, grandmother of Statira.

20. *Cohortanus*] referred to in Cotterell's translation of La Calprenède's *Cassandre* as Roxana's father, cousin-german of Darius, and governor of the Sacans; cf. II.45 n.

-13-

The Rival Queens,

or

the Death of Alexander the Great

ACT I

[I.i]

     Enter Hephestion, Lysimachus *fighting*, Clytus *parting them.*

CLYTUS.

    What, are you madmen! Ha!—Put up, I say—

    Then mischief in the bosoms of ye both.

LYSIMACHUS.

    I have his sword.

CLYTUS.   But must not have his life.

LYSIMACHUS.

    Must not, old Clytus?

CLYTUS.   Mad Lysimachus,

    You must not.

HEPHESTION.   Coward flesh! O feeble arm!   5

    He dallied with my point, and when I thrust,

    He frowned, and smiled, and foiled me like a fencer.

    O reverend Clytus, father of the war,

    Most famous guard of Alexander's life,

    Take pity on my youth, and lend a sword.   10

    Lysimachus is brave, and will not scorn me;

    Kill me, or let me fight with him again.

LYSIMACHUS.

    There, take thy sword; and since thou art resolved

    For death, thou hast the noblest from my hand.

---

1. say—] *Q 2–3;* say *Q 1.*   4–5. Mad . . . not.] *Q 1–3 print as*
2. Then] Then, *Q 1–3.*   *one line.*
4. not,] *Q 2–3;* not *Q 1.*

    1. *Put up*] sheathe your swords.

CLYTUS.

    Stay thee, Lysimachus; Hephestion, hold.   15
    I bar you both, my body interposed.
    Now let me see which of you dares to strike.
    By Jove, ye've stirred the old man. That rash arm
    That first advances, moves against the gods,
    Against the wrath of Clytus and the will   20
    Of our great king, whose deputy I stand.

LYSIMACHUS.

    Well, I shall take another time.

HEPHESTION.   And I.

CLYTUS.   'Tis false.

    Another time? What time? What foolish hour?
    No time shall see a brave man do amiss.
    And what's the noble cause that makes this madness?   25
    What big ambition blows this dangerous fire?
    A cupid's puff, is it not woman's breath?
    By all our triumphs in the heat of youth,
    When towns were sacked, and beauties prostrate lay,
    When my blood boiled, and nature worked me high,   30
    Clytus ne'er bowed his body to such shame.
    The brave will scorn their cobweb arts. The souls
    Of all that whining, smiling, coz'ning sex
    Weigh not one thought of any man of war.

LYSIMACHUS.

    I must confess our vengeance was ill-timed.   35

CLYTUS.

    Death! I had rather this right arm were lost,
    To which I owe my glory, than our king
    Should know your fault. What, on this famous day!

HEPHESTION.

    I was to blame.

CLYTUS.   This memorable day,

    When our hot master, that would tire the world,   40
    Outride the lab'ring sun, and tread the stars
    When he inclined to rest, comes peaceful on,

15. Lysimachus;] *Q7;* Lysimachus,
Q1-3

---

    32. *cobweb*] suggesting both "flimsy" and "ensnaring."
    33. *coz'ning*] cozening; deceiving.

List'ning to songs, while all his trumpets sleep,
And plays with monarchs whom he used to drive,
Shall we begin disorders, make new broils?   45
We that have temper learnt, shall we awake
Hushed Mars, the lion that had left to roar?

LYSIMACHUS.
'Tis true. Old Clytus is an oracle.
Put up, Hephestion. —Did not passion blind
My reason, I on such occasion too   50
Could thus have urged.

HEPHESTION.   Why is it then we love?

CLYTUS.
Because unmanned.—
Why, is not Alexander grown example?
O, that a face should thus bewitch a soul,
And ruin all that's right and reasonable.   55
Talk be my bane, yet the old man must talk:
Not so he loved when he at Issus fought,
And joined in mighty duel great Darius,
Whom from his chariot flaming all with gems
He hurled to earth and crushed th'imperial crown,   60
Nor could the gods defend their images
Which with the gaudy coach lay overturned.
'Twas not the shaft of love that did the feat,
Cupid had nothing there to do. But now
Two wives he takes, two rival queens disturb   65
The court; and while each hand does beauty hold,
Where is there room for glory?

HEPHESTION.   In his heart.

CLYTUS.   Well said.
You are his favorite, and I had forgot
Who I was talking to. See, Sysigambis comes
Reading a letter to your princess. Go,   70
Now make your claim, while I attend the king.   *Exit.*

Enter Sysigambis, Parisatis.

53. Why,] Why *Q 1–3.*

46. *temper*] self-control.
47. *left to roar*] left off roaring.
57. *Issus*] city in Cilicia where Alexander defeated Darius in 333 B.C.

PARISATIS.

    Did you not love my father? Yes, I see
    You did. His very name but mentioned brings
    The tears, howe'er unwilling, to your eyes.
    I loved him too. He would not thus have forced   75
    My trembling heart, which your commands may break,
    But never bend.

SYSIGAMBIS.   Forbear thy lost complaints,
    Urge not a suit which I can never grant.
    Behold the royal signet of the king;
    Therefore resolve to be Hephestion's wife.   80

PARISATIS.

    No, since Lysimachus has won my heart,
    My body shall be ashes ere another's.

SYSIGAMBIS.

    For sixty rolling years who ever stood
    The shock of state so unconcerned as I?
    This, whom I thought to govern being young,   85
    Heav'n, as a plague to power, has rendered strong.
    Judge my distresses and my temper prize,
    Who, though unfortunate, would still be wise.

LYSIMACHUS.

    To let you know that misery does sway   *Both kneel.*
    An humbler fate than yours, see at your feet   90
    The lost Lysimachus. O mighty queen,
    I have but this to beg, impartial stand;
    And since Hephestion serves by your permission,
    Disdain not me who ask your royal leave
    To cast a throbbing heart before her feet.   95

HEPHESTION.

    A blessing like possession of the princess,
    No services, not crowns, nor all the blood
    That circles in our bodies can deserve.
    Therefore I take all helps, much more the king's;
    And what your majesty vouchsafed to give,   100
    Your word, is passed, where all my hopes must hang.

101. word,] word *Q 1–3.*

---

85. *This*] i.e., Parisatis.
87. *prize*] estimate.

LYSIMACHUS.

    There perish too. All words want sense in love;
    But love and I bring such a perfect passion,
    So nobly pure, 'tis worthy of her eyes,
    Which without blushing she may justly prize.   105

HEPHESTION.

    Such arrogance, should Alexander woo,
    Would lose him all the conquest he has won.

LYSIMACHUS.

    Let not a conquest once be named by you,
    Who this dispute must to my mercy own.

SYSIGAMBIS.

    Rise, brave Lysimachus; Hephestion, rise.   110
    'Tis true Hephestion first declared his love;
    And 'tis as true I promised him my aid!
    Your glorious king turned mighty advocate.
    How noble therefore were the victory,
    If we could vanquish this disordered love.   115

HEPHESTION.

    'Twill never be.

LYSIMACHUS.   No, I will yet love on,
    And hear from Alexander's mouth, in what
    Hephestion merits more than I.

SYSIGAMBIS.   I grieve,
    And fear the boldness which your love inspires;
    But lest her sight should haste your enterprise,   120
    'Tis just I take the object from your eyes.

                            Exeunt Sysigambis, Parisatis.

LYSIMACHUS.

    She's gone, and see, the day, as if her look
    Had kindled it, is lost now she is vanished.

HEPHESTION.

    A sudden gloominess and horror comes
    About me.

LYSIMACHUS.   Let's away to meet the king.   125
    You know my suit.

110.   Lysimachus;] Lysimachus,
Q 1–3.

---

 109. *to . . . own*] acknowledge to be dependent on my mercy (?).

HEPHESTION.   Yonder Cassander comes.
   He may inform us.
LYSIMACHUS.   No, I would avoid him.
   There's something in that busy face of his
   That shocks my nature.
HEPHESTION.   Where and what you please.   *Exeunt.*

Enter Cassander.

CASSANDER.
   The morning rises black, the low'ring sun,   130
   As if the dreadful business he foreknew,
   Drives heavily his sable chariot on.
   The face of day now blushes scarlet deep,
   As if it feared the stroke which I intend,
   Like that of Jupiter—lightning and thunder.   135
   The lords above are angry and talk big,
   Or rather walk the mighty cirque like mourners
   Clad in long clouds, the robes of thickest night,
   And seem to groan for Alexander's fall.
   'Tis as Cassander's soul could wish it were,   140
   Which, whensoe'er it flies at lofty mischief,
   Would startle fate and make all heav'n concerned.
   A mad Chaldean in the dead of night
   Came to my bedside with a flaming torch,
   And bellowing o'er me like a spirit damned,   145
   He cried, "Well had it been for Babylon
   If cursed Cassander never had been born."

Enter Thessalus, Philip, *with letters.*

THESSALUS.
   My lord Cassander!
CASSANDER.   Ha! Who's there?
PHILIP.   Your friends.
CASSANDER.
   Welcome, dear Thessalus and brother Philip.
   Papers? With what contents?

---

   137. *cirque*] circus, amphitheater.
   143. *Chaldean*] native of Chaldea (province of Babylonia). The Chaldeans were noted for occult learning.

PHILIP   From Macedon   150
    A trusty slave arrived. Great Antipater
    Writes that your mother labored with you long,
    Your birth was slow, and slow is all your life.
CASSANDER.
    He writes, "Dispatch the king! Craterus comes,
    Who in my room must govern Macedon.   155
    Let him not live a day." —He dies tonight;
    And thus my father but forestalls my purpose.
    Why am I slow then? If I rode on thunder,
    I must a moment have to fall from heaven
    Ere I could blast the growth of this colossus.   160
THESSALUS.
    The haughty Polyperchon comes this way,
    A malcontent, one whom I lately wrought,
    That for a slight affront, at Susa giv'n,
    Bears Alexander most pernicious hate.
CASSANDER.
    So when I mocked the Persians that adored him,   165
    He strook me on the face, and by the hair
    He swung me to his guards to be chastised;
    For which, and for my father's weighty cause,
    When I abandon what I have resolved,
    May I again be beaten like a slave.   170

Enter Polyperchon.

    But lo, where Polyperchon comes. Now fire him
    With such complaints, that he may shoot to ruin.
POLYPERCHON.
    Sure I have found those friends dare second me;
    I hear fresh murmurs as I pass along,

150. Macedon] *C2;* Macedon,   170.1. *Enter* Polyperchon] *in Q 1–3*
Q 1–3.   *after l. 171.*
157. father] *Q 2–3;* father, *Q 1.*

154. *Craterus*] one of Alexander's generals, appointed to the regency of
Macedonia in place of Antipater in 324 B.C.
   155. *in my room*] instead of me.
   162. *wrought*] persuaded (insidiously).
   163. *Susa*] capital of Susiana, one of the chief provinces of the ancient
Persian empire.
   165. *adored*] paid divine honors to; i.e., prostrated themselves before.

Yet rather than put up, I'll do't alone. 175
Did not Pausanias, a youth, a stripling,
A beardless boy, swelled with inglorious wrong,
For a less cause his father Philip kill?
Peace then, full heart! Move like a cloud about,
And when time ripens thee to break, O, shed 180
The stock of all thy poison on his head.

CASSANDER.

All nations bow their heads with homage down
And kiss the feet of this exalted man;
The name, the shout, the blast from every mouth
Is Alexander. Alexander bursts 185
Your cheeks, and with a crack so loud
It drowns the voice of heaven. Like dogs ye fawn,
The earth's commanders fawn, and follow him;
Mankind starts up to hear his blasphemy,
And if this hunter of the barbarous world 190
But wind himself a god, you echo him
With universal cry.

POLYPERCHON.   I echo him?

I fawn, or fall like a fat eastern slave
And lick his feet? Boys hoot me from the palace
To haunt some cloister with my senseless walk, 195
When thus the noble soul of Polyperchon
Lets go the aim of all his actions, honor.

THESSALUS.

The king shall flay me, cut me up alive,
Ply me with fire and scourges, rack me worse
Than once he did Philotas, ere I bow. 200

CASSANDER.

Curse on thy tongue for mentioning Philotas.
I had rather thou hadst Aristander been,

---

176. *Pausanias*] a Macedonian youth who murdered Philip in 336 B.C.

178. *Philip*] Philip II, late King of Macedonia, Alexander's father.

191. *wind*] "trumpet"; proclaim as with the blast of a hunting horn.

192. *cry*] combines the ideas of a shouting crowd and of the yelping of hounds in the chase.

200. *Philotas*] one of Alexander's commanders, who was tortured and put to death in 330 B.C. on suspicion of having plotted against Alexander's life.

And to my soul's confusion raised up hell
With all the furies brooding upon horrors,
Than brought Philotas's murder to remembrance.   205
PHILIP.
   I saw him racked. A sight so dismal sad
My eyes did ne'er behold.
CASSANDER.   So dismal! Peace,
   It is unutterable. Let me stand
And think upon the tragedy you saw.
By Mars, it comes; ay, now the rack's set forth,   210
Bloody Craterus, his inveterate foe,
With pitiless Hephestion standing by.
Philotas, like an angel seized by fiends,
Is straight disrobed, a napkin ties his head,
His warlike arms with shameful cords are bound,   215
And every slave can now the valiant wound.
POLYPERCHON.
   Now, by the soul of royal Philip fled,
I dare pronounce young Alexander, who
Would be a god, is cruel as a devil.
CASSANDER.
   O, Polyperchon, Philip, Thessalus,   220
Did not your eyes rain blood, your spirits burst,
To see your noble fellow-soldier burn,
Yet without trembling or a tear endure
The torments of the damned? O barbarians,
Could you stand by, and yet refuse to suffer?   225
Ye saw him bruised, torn, to the bones made bare;
His veins wide lanced, and the poor, quivering flesh
With pincers from his manly bosom ripped,
Till ye discovered the great heart lie panting.
POLYPERCHON.
   Why killed we not the king to save Philotas?   230
CASSANDER.
   Asses! Fools! But asses will bray, and fools be angry.
Why stood ye then like statues? There's the case.

---

214. *napkin*] small piece of cloth.
216. *valiant*] brave man.

The horror of the sight had turned ye marble.
So the pale Trojans from their weeping walls
Saw the dear body of the godlike Hector,   235
Bloody and soiled, dragged on the famous ground,
Yet senseless stood, nor with drawn weapons ran
To save the great remains of that prodigious man.

PHILIP.

Wretched Philotas! Bloody Alexander!

THESSALUS.

Soon after him the great Parmenio fell,   240
Stabbed in his orchard by the tyrant's doom;
But where's the need to mention public loss,
When each receives particular disgrace?

POLYPERCHON.

Late I remember, to a banquet called,
After Alcides' goblet swift had gone   245
The giddy round, and wine had made me bold,
Stirring the spirits up to talk with kings,
I saw Craterus with Hephestion enter
In Persian robes. To Alexander's health
They largely drank, then, turning eastward, fell   250
Flat on the pavement and adored the sun.
Straight to the king they sacred reverence gave
With solemn words, "O son of thund'ring Jove,
Young Ammon, live forever!" then kissed the ground.
I laughed aloud, and, scoffing, asked 'em why   255
They kissed no harder. But the king leapt up
And spurned me to the earth with this reply,
"Do thou!" whilst with his foot he pressed my neck
Till from my ears, my nose, and mouth the blood
Gushed forth, and I lay foaming on the earth,   260
For which I wish this dagger in his heart.

---

240. *Parmenio*] one of Alexander's generals, father of Philotas. He was
assassinated on Alexander's orders after the execution of Philotas.

243. *particular*] private.

245. *Alcides*] Hercules. Plutarch mentions a report that Alexander died
after drinking a "bowl of Heracles"; see Plutarch's *Lives* (Loeb Library),
VII, 433.

250. *largely*] abundantly.

254. *Young Ammon*] i.e., son of Jupiter Ammon; see note to Dedicatory
Epistle, l. 12.

CASSANDER.

    There spoke the spirit of Callisthenes.
    Remember he's a man, his flesh as soft
    And penetrable as a girl's. We have seen him wounded,
    A stone has struck him, yet no thunderbolt.   265
    A pebble felled this Jupiter along,
    A sword has cut him, a javelin pierced him,
    Water will drown him, fire burn him,
    A surfeit, nay, a fit of common sickness
    Brings this immortal to the gate of death.   270

POLYPERCHON.

    Why should we more delay the glorious business?
    Are your hearts firm?

PHILIP.   Hell cannot be more bent
    To any ruin than I to the king's.

THESSALUS.   And I.

POLYPERCHON.

    Behold my hand, and if you doubt my truth,
    Tear up my breast and lay my heart upon it.   275

CASSANDER.

    Join them, O worthy, hearty, noble hands,
    Fit instruments for such majestic souls;
    Remember Hermolaus, and be hushed.

POLYPERCHON.

    Still as the bosom of the desert night,
    As fatal planets, or deep plotting fiends.   280

CASSANDER.

    Today he comes to Babylon from Susa
    With proud Roxana. —Ha! Who's that? —Look here!

---

269. common sickness] *Q2–3;* common-sickness *Q1.*
281. to Babylon from] *S-C;* from Babylon to *Q1–3.*

282. With . . . here.] *Q1–3 print as two lines:* With . . . Roxana./ Ha! . . . here.

---

262. *Callisthenes*] philospher who accompanied Alexander on his expedition, criticized his adoption of oriental customs, and was executed after being accused of inciting Hermolaus and other pages to rebel.
266. *along*] at full length.
276. *hearty*] courageous.
278. *Hermolaus*] a Macedonian youth who led Alexander's pages in a conspiracy and was executed in 327 B.C.
280. *fatal*] determining men's fates.

Enter the ghost of King Philip, *shaking a truncheon at them.* [*It*] *walks over the stage.*

> Now, by the gods, or furies, which I ne'er
> Believed, there's one of 'em arrived to shake us.
> What art thou? Glaring thing, speak. What! The spirit   285
> Of our King Philip, or of Polyphemus?
> Nay, hurl thy truncheon, second it with thunder,
> We will abide.—   [*Exit ghost.*]
> > Thessalus, saw you nothing?

THESSALUS.

> Yes, and am more amazed than you can be.

PHILIP.

> 'Tis said that many prodigies were seen   290
> This morn, but none so horrible as this.

POLYPERCHON.

> What can you fear? Though the earth yawned so wide
> That all the labors of the deep were seen,
> And Alexander stood on th'other side,
> I'd leap the burning ditch to give him death,   295
> Or sink myself forever. Pray, to the business.

CASSANDER.

> As I was saying, this Roxana, whom,
> To aggravate my hate to him, I love,
> Meeting him as he came triumphant from
> The Indies, kept him reveling at Susa;   300
> But as I found, a deep repentance since
> Turns his affections to the Queen Statira,
> To whom he swore, before he could espouse her,
> That he would never bed Roxana more.

POLYPERCHON.

> How did the Persian queens receive the news   305
> Of his revolt?

THESSALUS.   With grief incredible.

> Great Sysigambis wept, but the young queen

282.1. *them*] *'em Q1–3.*   296. Pray,] *Q2–3;* pray *Q1.*
284. 'em] *Q1;* them *Q2–3.*   298. him,] *Q2–3;* him *Q1.*
294. th'other] *Q1;* the other *Q2–3.*

---

286 *Polyphemus*] a Cyclops, a one-eyed, man-eating giant.
287. *second it*] back it up.
306. *revolt*] change of allegiance.

Fell dead amongst her maids; nor could their care,
With richest cordials, for an hour or more,
Recover life.

CASSANDER.   Knowing how much she loved,   310
I hoped to turn her all into Medea;
For when the first gust of her grief was past,
I entered, and with breath prepared did blow
The dying sparks into a tow'ring flame,
Describing the new love he bears Roxana,   315
Conceiving not unlikely that the line
Of dead Darius in her cause might rise.
Is any panther's, lioness's rage
So furious, any torrent's fall so swift
As a wronged woman's hate? Thus far it helps   320
To give him troubles; which perhaps may end him
And set the court in universal uproar.
But see, it ripens more than I expected,
The scene works up: kill him, or kill thyself;
So there be mischief any way, 'tis well.   325
Now change the vizor, everyone disperse,
And with a face of friendship meet the king.   *Exeunt.*

[I.ii]   *Enter* Sysigambis, Statira, Parisatis, *attendants.*

STATIRA.

Give me a knife, a draught of poison, flames;
Swell, heart; break, break, thou stubborn thing.
Now, by the sacred fire, I'll not be held;
Why do you wish me life, yet stifle me
For want of air? Pray give me leave to walk.   5

SYSIGAMBIS.

Is there no reverence to my person due?
Darius would have heard me. Trust not rumor.

308. Fell . . . care] *S-C; Q1–3 print*   [I.ii]
as two lines: Fell . . . maids,/ Nor . . .   4. you] *Q1;* ye *Q2–3.*
care.   7. me.] me: *Q2–3;* me, *Q1.*
321. troubles;] *Q2–3;* troubles *Q1.*

311. *Medea*] wife of Jason, who, when deserted by him, murdered their
children and his new wife.
326 *vizor*] vizard; face-mask.

STATIRA.

No, he hates,
He loathes the beauties which he has enjoyed.
O, he is false, that great, that glorious man   10
Is tyrant midst of his triumphant spoils,
Is bravely false to all the gods, forsworn.
Yet who would think it? No, it cannot be,
It cannot. What, that dear, protesting man!
He that has warmed my feet with thousand sighs,   15
Then cooled 'em with his tears, died on my knees,
Outwept the morning with his dewy eyes,
And groaned and swore the wond'ring stars away?

SYSIGAMBIS.

No, 'tis impossible; believe thy mother
That knows him well.

STATIRA.   Away, and let me die.   20
O, 'tis my fondness, and my easy nature
That would excuse him; but I know he's false,
'Tis now the common talk, the news o'th' world,
False to Statira, false to her that loved him.
That loved him, cruel victor as he was,   25
And took him bathed all o'er in Persian blood,
Kissed the dear, cruel wounds, and washed 'em o'er
And o'er in tears; then bound 'em with my hair,
Laid him all night upon my panting bosom,
Lulled like a child, and hushed him with my songs.   30

PARISATIS.

If this be true, ah, who will ever trust
A man again?

STATIRA.   A man! A man! My Parisatis,
Thus with thy hand held up, thus let me swear thee.
By the eternal body of the sun,
Whose body, O, forgive the blasphemy,   35
I loved not half so well as the least part
Of my dear, precious, faithless Alexander;
For I will tell thee, and to warn thee of him,

18. groaned] *Q2–3;* groaned, *Q1.*   32. A man! A man!] *Q2–3;* A man!
25. him] *Q1;* me *Q2–3.*   A man, *Q1.*

16. *died*] languished with passion.
21. *fondness*] foolish love.

Not the spring's mouth, nor breath of jessamine,
Nor violets' infant sweets, nor opening buds   40
Are half so sweet as Alexander's breast;
From every pore of him a perfume falls,
He kisses softer than a southern wind,
Curls like a vine, and touches like a god.

SYSIGAMBIS.

When will thy spirits rest, these transports cease?   45

STATIRA.

Will you not give me leave to warn my sister?
As I was saying—but I told his sweetness.
Then he will talk, good gods, how he will talk!
Even when the joy he sighed for is possessed,
He speaks the kindest words and looks such things,   50
Vows with such passion, swears with so much grace,
That 'tis a kind of heaven to be deluded by him.

PARISATIS.

But what was it that you would have me swear?

STATIRA.

Alas, I had forgot. Let me walk by
And weep awhile, and I shall soon remember.   55

                                    [*Retires and kneels.*]

SYSIGAMBIS.

Have patience, child, and give her liberty;
Passions like seas will have their ebbs and flows.
Yet while I see her thus, not all the losses
We have received since Alexander's conquest
Can touch my hardened soul; her sorrow reigns   60
Too fully there.

PARISATIS.   But what if she should kill herself?

STATIRA.

Roxana then enjoys my perjured love.
Roxana clasps my monarch in her arms,
Dotes on my conqueror, my dear lord, my king,
Devours my lips, eats him with hungry kisses.   65

40. infant   sweets]   *Q 1;*   infant-   65. my] *Q 1–3;* his *C2, S-C.*
sweets *Q 2–3.*

---

40. *sweets*] scents.
65. *my lips*] Lee may have wished to suggest Statira's possessiveness towards Alexander; but see textual note.

-29-

She grasps him all, she, the curst happy she.
By heav'n, I cannot bear it, 'tis too much.   *Rises.*
I'll die, or rid me of the burning torture.
I will have remedy, I will, I will,
Or go distracted; madness may throw off   70
The mighty load, and drown the flaming passion.
Madam, draw near, with all that are in presence,
And listen to the vow which here I make.

SYSIGAMBIS.
Take heed, my dear Statira, and consider
What desperate love enforces you to swear.   75

STATIRA.
Pardon me, for I have considered well;
And here I bid adieu to all mankind.
Farewell, ye coz'ners of the easy sex,
And thou, the greatest, falsest, Alexander;
Farewell, thou most beloved, thou faithless dear.   80
If I but mention him, the tears will fall.
Sure there is not a letter in his name
But is a charm to melt a woman's eyes.

SYSIGAMBIS.
Clear up thy griefs. Thy king, thy Alexander,
Comes on to Babylon.

STATIRA.   Why, let him come,   85
Joy of all eyes but the forlorn Statira's.

SYSIGAMBIS.
Wilt thou not see him?

STATIRA.   By heav'n, I never will.
That is my vow, my sacred resolution;
And when I break it—   *Kneels.*

SYSIGAMBIS.   Ah, do not ruin all.

STATIRA.
May I again be flattered and deluded,   90
May sudden death, and horrid, come instead
Of what I wish, and take me unprepared.

SYSIGAMBIS.
Still kneel, and with the same breath call again
The woeful imprecation thou hast made.

88. That] *Q1;* This *Q2–3.*

---

78. *easy*] compliant, credulous.
93. *again*] back.

STATIRA.

No, I will publish it through all the court,   95
Then in the bowers of great Semiramis
Forever lock my woes from human view.

SYSIGAMBIS.

Yet be persuaded.

STATIRA.   Never urge me more,
Lest, driv'n to rage, I should my life abhor,
And in your presence put an end to all   100
The fast calamities that round me fall.

PARISATIS.

O angry heav'n, what have the guiltless done?
And where shall wretched Parisatis run?

SYSIGAMBIS.

Captives in war, our bodies we resigned,
But now made free, love does our spirits bind.   105

STATIRA.

When to my purposed loneness I retire,   ⎫
Your sight I through the grates shall oft desire, ⎬
And after Alexander's health enquire.   ⎭
And if this passion cannot be removed,   ⎫
Ask how my resolution he approved,   ⎬   110
How much he loves, how much he is beloved.   ⎭
Then when I hear that all things please him well,
Thank the good gods, and hide me in my cell.   *Exeunt.*

---

96. *bowers . . . Semiramis*] the hanging gardens of Babylon, supposed to
have been erected by Queen Semiramis, mythical founder of the Assyrian
empire of Nineveh.

ACT II

Noise of trumpets sounding far off.

The scene draws and discovers a battle of crows or ravens in the air. An eagle and a dragon meet and fight. The eagle drops down with all the rest of the birds, and the dragon flies away. Soldiers walk off shaking their heads. The conspirators[, Cassander, Polyperchon, Philip, *and* Thessalus,] *come forward.*

CASSANDER.

    He comes. The fatal glory of the world,
    The headlong Alexander with a guard
    Of thronging crowns comes on to Babylon,
    Though warned, in spite of all the pow'rs above,
    Who by these prodigies foretell his ruin.   5

POLYPERCHON.

    Why all this noise because a king must die?
    Or does heav'n fear, because he swayed the earth,
    His ghost will war with the high thunderer?
    Curse on the babbling fates that cannot see
    A great man tumble, but they must be talking.   10

CASSANDER.

    The spirit of King Philip, in those arms
    We saw him wear, passed groaning through the court,
    His dreadful eyeballs rolled their horror upwards,
    He waved his arms, and shook his wondrous head.
    I've heard that at the crowing of the cock   15
    Lions will roar and goblings steal away;
    But this majestic air stalks steadfast on
    Spite of the morn that calls him from the east,
    Nor minds the op'ning of the iv'ry door.

    0.2. *The scene . . . discovers*] i.e., the painted shutters are drawn apart to reveal.

    0.2–4. *a battle . . . away*] The Restoration stages were furnished with crane mechanisms for elaborate flight effects.

    0.5–6. *come forward*] i.e., from the scenic area behind the proscenium on to the large apron.

    16. *goblings*] goblins.

    17. *air*] In III.231 Lee clearly uses the word in the sense of "spirit, ghost." Here that meaning appears to be combined with the more common sense of "mien, appearance."

PHILIP.

    'Tis certain there was never day like this.   20

CASSANDER.

    Late as I musing walked behind the palace,
    I met a monstrous child that, with his hands,
    Held to his face, which seemed all over eyes,
    A silver bowl, and wept it full of blood.
    But having spied me, like a cockatrice   25
    He glared awhile; then, with a shriek so shrill
    As all the winds had whistled from his mouth,
    He dashed me with the gore he held, and vanished.

POLYPERCHON.

    That which befell me, though 'twas horrid, yet
    When I consider, it appears ridiculous;   30
    For, as I passed through a bye vacant place,
    I met two women very old and ugly
    That wrung their hands, and howled, and beat their breasts,
    And cried out, "Poison!" When I asked the cause,
    They took me by the ears, and with strange force   35
    Held me to earth, then laughed and disappeared.

CASSANDER.

    O, how I love destruction with a method
    Which none discern but those that weave the plot.
    Like silkworms we are hid in our own weft,
    But we shall burst at last through all the strings,   40
    And when time calls, come forth in a new form:
    Not insects to be trod, but dragons winged.

THESSALUS.

    The face of all the court is strangely altered.
    There's not a Persian I can meet but stares
    As if he were distracted. Oxyartes,   45
    Statira's uncle, openly declaimed
    Against the perjury of Alexander.

---

30. consider,] *Q 2–3;* consider *Q 1.*   36. to earth] *Q 1;* to the earth
                                                   Q 2–3.

---

25. *cockatrice*] basilisk; mythical reptile able to kill with its glance.
31. *bye*] off the main track.
39. *weft*] something spun or woven.
45. *Oxyartes*] a Bactrian prince, historically the father of Roxana.

PHILIP.

    Others, more fearful, are removed to Susa,
    Dreading Roxana's rage, who comes i'th' rear
    To Babylon.

CASSANDER.   It glads my rising soul   50
    That we shall see him racked before he dies.
    I know he loves Statira more than life,
    And on a crowd of kings in triumph borne
    Comes, big with expectation, to enjoy her.
    But when he hears the oaths which she has ta'en,   55
    Her last adieu made public to the world,
    Her vowed divorce, how will remorse consume him,
    Prey, like the bird of hell, upon his liver!

POLYPERCHON.

    To balk his longing and delude his lust
    Is more than death, 'tis earnest for damnation.   60

CASSANDER.

    Then comes Roxana, who must help our party;
    I know her jealous, bloody, and ambitious.
    Sure 'twas the likeness of her heart to mine
    And sympathy of natures caused me love her.
    'Tis fixed, I must enjoy her, and no way   65
    So proper as to make her guilty first.

POLYPERCHON.

    To see two rival queens of different humors
    With a variety of torments vex him.

           Enter Lysimachus, Hephestion.

CASSANDER.

    Of that anon. But see, Lysimachus
    And the young favorite. Sort, sort yourselves,   70
    And like to other mercenary souls
    Adore this mortal god that soon must bleed.

LYSIMACHUS.

    Here I will wait the king's approach, and stand
    His utmost anger if he do me wrong.

---

    54. *big*] swollen.
    58. *bird of hell*] presumably the vulture which tore continuously at the
liver of Prometheus (in the Caucasian mountains).
    70. *sort yourselves*] separate into your positions.

HEPHESTION.

    That cannot be, from power so absolute   75
    And high as his.

LYSIMACHUS.   Well, you and I have done.

POLYPERCHON.

    How the court thickens!   *Trumpets sound.*

CASSANDER.

    Nothing to what it will. Does he not come
    To hear a thousand thousand embassies,
    Which from all parts to Babylon are brought,   80
    As if the parliament of the whole world
    Had met, and he came on, a god, to give
    The infinite assembly glorious audience.

      Enter Clytus; Aristander *in his robes, with a wand.*

ARISTANDER.

    Haste, reverend Clytus, haste, and stop the king.

CLYTUS.

    He is already entered. Then the press   85
    Of princes that attend so thick about him
    Keep all that would approach at certain distance.

ARISTANDER.

    Though he were hemmed with deities, I'd speak to him,
    And turn him back from this highway to death.

CLYTUS.

    Here place yourself, within his trumpets' sound.   90

      [Enter Eumenes, *priests, etc.]*

    Lo, the Chaldean priests appear. Behold
    The sacred fire, Nearchus and Eumenes
    With their white wands and dressed in eastern robes
    To soothe the king, who loves the Persian mode.
    But see, the master of the world appears.   95

      Enter Alexander. *All kneel but* Clytus.

HEPHESTION.

    O son of Jupiter, live forever.

89. highway] *Q1;* high way *Q2–3.*　91. Chaldean] *Q2–3;* Caldean *Q1.*

85. *press*] throng.
92. *Nearchus*] historically, commander of Alexander's fleet.

ALEXANDER.

 Rise all, and thou, my second self, my love,
 O my Hephestion, raise thee from the earth
 Up to my breast, and hide thee in my heart.
 Art thou grown cold? Why hang thine arms at distance? 100
 Hug me, or else, by heaven, thou lov'st me not.

HEPHESTION.

 Not love, my lord? Break not the heart you framed
 And molded up to such an excellence,
 Then stamped on it your own immortal image.
 Not love the king? Such is not woman's love, 105
 So fond a friendship, such a sacred flame
 As I must doubt to find in breasts above.

ALEXANDER.

 Thou dost, thou lov'st me, crown of all my wars,
 Thou dearer to me than my groves of laurel,
 I know thou lov'st thy Alexander more 110
 Than Clytus does the king. No tears, Hephestion,
 I read thy passion in thy manly eyes,
 And glory in those planets of my life
 Above the rival lights that shine in heaven.

LYSIMACHUS [aside].

 I see that death must wait me, yet I'll on. 115

ALEXANDER.

 I'll tell thee, friend, and mark it, all ye princes,
 Though never mortal man arrived to such
 A height as I, yet I would forfeit all,
 Cast all my purples and my conquered crowns,
 And die to save this darling of my soul. 120
 Give me thy hand, share all my scepters while
 I live; and when my hour of fate is come,
 I leave thee what thou meritest more than I, the world.

LYSIMACHUS.

 Dread sir, I cast me at your royal feet.

---

116. it,] Q4; it Q1–3.

 113. *planets . . . life*] i.e., orbs which, like planets, influence the course of my life.
 114. *lights*] includes two senses: (1) heavenly bodies; (2) eyes.
 119. *purples*] purple robes signifying imperial office.

II

ALEXANDER.

    What, my Lysimachus, whose veins are rich   125
    With our illustrious blood? My kinsman, rise.
    Is not that Clytus?

CLYTUS.   Your old faithful soldier.

ALEXANDER.

    Come to my hands; thus double arm the king.
    And now methinks I stand like the dread god
    Who, while his priests and I quaffed sacred blood,   130
    Acknowledged me his son. My lightning thou;
    And thou my mighty thunder. I have seen
    Thy glittering sword outfly celestial fire;
    And when I cried, "Begone and execute!"
    I've seen him run swifter than starting hinds,   135
    Nor bent the tender grass beneath his feet,
    Swifter than shadows fleeting o'er the fields,
    Nay, even the winds, with all their stock of wings,
    Have puffed behind, as wanting breath to reach him.

LYSIMACHUS.

    But if your majesty—

CLYTUS.   Who would not lose   140
    The last dear drop of blood for such a king?

ALEXANDER.

    Witness, my elder brothers of the sky,
    How much I love a soldier. —O my Clytus,
    Was it not when we passed the Granicus
    Thou didst preserve me from unequal force?   145
    It was when Spithridates and Rhesaces
    Fell both upon me with two dreadful strokes
    And clove my tempered helmet quite in sunder;
    Then, I remember, then thou didst me service.
    I think my thunder split him to the navel.   150

CLYTUS.

    To your great self you owe that victory,
    And sure your arms did never gain a nobler.

---

129. *god*] Jupiter Ammon.
144. *Granicus*] river in Mysia, where Alexander fought the decisive battle for entry into Asia in 334 B.C.
146. *Spithridates and Rhesaces*] Persian generals.

ALEXANDER.

By heaven, they never did, for well thou knowest,
And I am prouder to have passed that stream
Than that I drove a million o'er the plain.   155
Can none remember? yes, I know all must,
When glory, like the dazzling eagle, stood
Perched on my beaver in the Granic flood;
When fortune's self my standard trembling bore,
And the pale fates stood frighted on the shore;   160
When the immortals on the billows rode,
And I myself appeared the leading god.

ARISTANDER.

But all the honors which your youth has won
Are lost unless you fly from Babylon.
Haste with your chiefs, to Susa take your way,   165
Fly for your life, destructive is your stay.
This morning, having viewed the angry sky
And marked the prodigies that threatened high,
To our bright god I did for succor fly;
But, O—

ALEXANDER.   What fears thy reverend bosom shake?   170
Or dost thou from some dream of horror wake?
If so, come grasp me with thy shaking hand,
Or fall behind while I the danger stand.

ARISTANDER.

To Orosmades' cave I did repair
Where I atoned the dreadful god with prayer.   175
But as I prayed, I heard long groans within,
And shrieks, as of the damned that howl for sin.
I knew the omen, and I feared to stay,
But prostrate on the trembling pavement lay.
When he bodes happiness, he answers mild;   180
'Twas so of old, and the great image smiled.
But now in abrupt thunder he replied,

170. O—] Q2-3; O. Q1.

---

158. *beaver*] lower portion of the face-guard of a helmet (which could be
pushed up over the top of the helmet).

174. *Orosmades*] Ormazd or *Ahura Mazda* (the "wise lord"); the supreme
god of the Zoroastrian religious system.

180. *bodes*] predicts.

Loud as rent rocks or roaring seas he cried,
"All empire's crown, glory of Babylon,
Whose head stands wrapped in clouds, must tumble down." 185

ALEXANDER.

If Babylon must fall, what is't to me?
Or can I help immutable decree?
Down then, vast frame, with all thy lofty towers,
Since 'tis so ordered by almighty powers.
Pressed by the fates, unloose your golden bars;   190
'Tis great to fall the envy of the stars.

Enter Perdiccas, Meleager.

MELEAGER.

O, horror!

PERDICCAS.   Dire portents!

ALEXANDER.   Out with 'em then.
What, are you ghosts, ye empty shapes of men?
If so, the mysteries of hell unfold,
Be all the scrolls of destiny unrolled,   195
Open the brazen leaves, and let it come,
Point with a thunderbolt your monarch's doom.

PERDICCAS.

As Meleager and myself in field
Your Persian horse about the army wheeled,
We heard a noise, as of a rushing wind,   200
And a thick storm the eye of day did blind.
A croaking noise resounded through the air,
We looked, and saw big ravens battling there.
Each bird of night appeared himself a cloud,
They met and fought, and their wounds rained black blood. 205

MELEAGER.

All, as for honor, did their lives expose;
Their talons clashed, and beaks gave mighty blows,

184. empire's] empires *Q 1–3.*   193. you] *Q 1;* ye *Q 2–3.*
193. What,] *Q 2–3;* What *Q 1.*   195. unrolled,] *C1;* unrolled? *Q 1–3.*

184. *empire*] supreme political dominion.
198. *in field*] engaged in military exercises.
199. *horse*] cavalry.

Whilst dreadful sounds did our scared sense assail,
As of small thunder or huge Scythian hail.

PERDICCAS.

    Our augurs shook when with a horrid groan   210
We thought that all the clouds had tumbled down.
Soldiers and chiefs, who can the wonder tell,
Strook to the ground, promiscuously fell,
While the dark birds, each pond'rous as a shield,
For fifty furlongs hid the fatal field.   215

ALEXANDER.

    Be witness for me, all ye powers divine,
If ye be angry, 'tis no fault of mine.
Therefore let furies face me with a band
From hell, my virtue shall not make a stand;
Though all the curtains of the sky be drawn,   220
And the stars wink, young Ammon shall go on;
While my Statira shines, I cannot stray, ⎫
Love lifts his torch to light me on my way, ⎬
And her bright eyes create another day. ⎭

LYSIMACHUS.

    Ere you remove, be pleased, dread sir, to hear   225
A prince allied to you by blood.

ALEXANDER.   Speak quickly.

LYSIMACHUS.

    For all that I have done for you in war,
I beg the Princess Parisatis.

ALEXANDER.   Ha!
    Is not my word already passed? Hephestion,
I know he hates thee, but he shall not have her.   230
We heard of this before. —Lysimachus,
I here command you nourish no design

232. command] *Q3;* command,
Q 1–2.

_____

   209. *Scythian hail*] In *Gloriana*, I, 24, Lee refers to the "Northern climate of the Scythians."
   212–213.] i.e., common soldiers and officers, who are able to recount the wonderful event, fell indiscriminately (regardless of rank) when they were struck to the ground.
   219. *virtue*] valor.
   219. *make a stand*] halt.

To prejudice my person in the man
I love, and will prefer to all the world.

LYSIMACHUS.

I never failed to obey your majesty,   235
Whilst you commanded what was in my power,
Nor could Hephestion fly more swift to serve,
When you commanded us to storm a town
Or fetch a standard from the enemy;
But when you charge me not to love the princess,   240
I must confess, I disobey you, as
I would the gods themselves, should they command.

ALEXANDER.

You should, brave sir, hear me, and then be dumb.
When by my order curst Callisthenes
Was as a traitor doomed to live in torments,   245
Your pity sped him in despite of me.
Think not I have forgot your insolence;
No, though I pardoned it, yet if again
Thou dar'st to cross me with another crime,
The bolts of fury shall be doubled on thee.   250
In the meantime think not of Parisatis;
For if thou dost, by Jupiter Ammon,
By my own head, and by King Philip's soul,
I'll not respect that blood of mine thou shar'st,
But use thee as the vilest Macedonian.   255

LYSIMACHUS.

I doubted not at first but I should meet
Your indignation, yet my soul's resolved,
And I shall never quit so brave a prize,
While I can draw a bow or lift a sword.

ALEXANDER.

Against my life, ha? Was it so? How now?   260
'Tis said that I am rash, of hasty humor;
But I appeal to the immortal gods
If ever petty, poor, prinvincial lord
Had temper like to mine? My slave, whom I
Could tread to clay, dares utter bloody threats.   265

---

245. *doomed*] sentenced.
246. *sped*] assisted.
255. *vilest*] of lowest birth.

CLYTUS.

    Contain yourself, dread sir. The noble prince,
    I see it in his countenance, would die
    To justify his truth, but love makes many faults.

LYSIMACHUS.

    I meant his minion there should feel my arm.
    Love asks his blood, nor shall he live to laugh   270
    At my destruction.

ALEXANDER.   Now be thy own judge.
    I pardon thee for my old Clytus's sake;
    But if once more thou mention thy rash love,
    Or dar'st attempt Hephestion's precious life,
    I'll pour such storms of indignation on thee,   275
    Philotas' rack, Callisthenes' disgrace,
    Shall be delight to what thou shalt endure.

               Enter Sysigambis, Parisatis.

HEPHESTION.

    My lord, the queen comes to congratulate
    Your safe arrival.

ALEXANDER.   O thou best of women,
    Source of my joy, blest parent of my love.   280

SYSIGAMBIS.

    Permit me kneel, and give those adorations
    Which from the Persian family are due.
    Have you not raised us from our ruins high,
    And when no hand could help, nor any eye
    Behold us with a tear, yours pitied me.   285
    You, like a god, snatched us from sorrow's gulf,
    Fixed us in thrones above our former state.

PARISATIS.

    Which, when a soul forgets, advanced so nobly,
    May it be drowned in deeper misery.

ALEXANDER.

    To meet me thus was generously done;   290
    But still there wants to crown my happiness,
    Life of my empire, treasure of my soul,

---

268. *truth*] loyalty.
278. *congratulate*] "express sympathetic joy on the occasion of" (*OED*).
291. *wants*] lacks.

My dear Statira! O, that heavenly beam,
Warmth of my brain, and firer of my heart;
Had she but shot to see me, had she met me,   295
By this time I had been amongst the gods,
If any ecstasy can make a height,
Or any rapture hurl us to the heavens.
CLYTUS [aside].

Now, who shall dare to tell him the queen's vow?
ALEXANDER.

How fares my love? Ha! —Neither answer me!   300
Ye raise my wonder. Darkness overwhelm me
If royal Sysigambis does not weep.
Trembling and horror pierce me cold as ice.
Is she not well? What, none, none answer me?
Or is it worse? Keep down, ye rising sighs,   305
And murmur in the hollow of my breast,
Run to my heart, and gather more sad wind,
That when the voice of fate shall call you forth,
Ye may, at one rush, from the seat of life
Blow the blood out, and burst me like a bladder.   310
HEPHESTION.

I would relate it, but my courage fails me.
ALEXANDER.

If she be dead—that if's impossible;
And let none here affirm it for his soul.
For he that dares but think so damned a lie,
I'll have his body straight impaled before me,   315
And glut my eyes upon his bleeding entrails.
CASSANDER [aside].

How will this engine of unruly passion
Roar when we have rammed him to the mouth with poison.
ALEXANDER.

Why stand you all as you were rooted here,
Like senseless trees, while to the stupid grove   320
I, like a wounded lion, groan my griefs,
And none will answer. —What, not my Hephestion?

---

317. *engine*] machine used in warfare.
318. *rammed . . . mouth*] i.e., as a charge into a gun.
320. *stupid*] "destitute of sensation, consciousness, thought or feeling"
(*OED*).

If thou hast any love for Alexander,
If ever I obliged thee by my care
When my quick sight has watched thee in the war,   325
Or if to see thee bleed I sent forth cries,
And, like a mother, washed thee with my tears;
If this be true, if I deserve thy love,
Ease me, and tell the cause of my disaster.

HEPHESTION.

Your mourning queen (which I had told before,   330
Had you been calm) has no disease but sorrow,
Which was occasioned first by jealous pangs.
She heard (for what can 'scape a watchful lover?)
That you at Susa, breaking all your vows,
Relapsed, and conquered by Roxana's charms,   335
Gave up yourself devoted to her arms.

ALEXANDER.

I know that subtle creature in my riot,
My reason gone, seduced me to her bed;
But when I waked, I shook the Circe off,
Though that enchantress held me by the arm,   340
And wept, and gazed with all the force of love;
Nor grieved I less for that which I had done
That when at Thais' suit, enraged with wine,
I set the famed Persepolis on fire.

HEPHESTION.

Your Queen Statira took it so to heart   345
That in the agony of love she swore
Never to see your majesty again;
With dreadful imprecations she confirmed
Her oath, and I much fear that she will keep it.

ALEXANDER.

Ha! Did she swear? Did that sweet creature swear?   350
I'll not believe it; no, she is all softness,
All melting, mild, and calm as a rocked infant,

351. it;] *C2;* it, *Q 1–3.*

_____

337. *subtle*] crafty.
337. *riot*] debauchery.
339. *Circe*] enchantress who turned men into animals.
343. *Thais*] Athenian courtesan, at whose instigation, after a drunken feast, Alexander set fire to the palace of Persepolis, the Persian capital.

Nor can you wake her into cries. By heaven,
She is the child of love, and she was born in smiles.
PARISATIS.
    I and my weeping mother heard her swear.   355
SYSIGAMBIS.
    And with such fierceness she did aggravate
The foulness of your fault, that I could wish
Your majesty would blot her from your breast.
ALEXANDER.
    Blot her? Forget her? Hurl her from my bosom
Forever, lose the star that gilds my life,   360
Guide of my days and goddess of my nights!
No, she shall stay with me in spite of vows,
My soul and body both are twisted with her.
The god of love empties his golden quiver,
Shoots every grain of her into my heart.   365
She is all mine, by heaven, I feel her here
Panting and warm, the dearest, O Statira!
SYSIGAMBIS.
    Have patience, son, and trust to heaven and me.
If my authority, or the remembrance
Of dead Darius, or her mother's soul   370
Can work upon her, she again is yours.
ALEXANDER.
    O mother, help me, help your wounded son,
And move the soul of my offended dear.
But fly, haste, ere the sad procession's made.
Spend not a thought in a reply. Begone,   375
If you would have me live—and Parisatis,
Hang thou about her knees, wash 'em with tears.
Nay, haste. The breath of gods and eloquence
Of angels go along with you—O, my heart!

                        Exeunt Sysigambis *and* Parisatis.
LYSIMACHUS.
    Now let your majesty, who feel the torments   380
And sharpest pangs of love, encourage mine.
ALEXANDER.
    Ha—

353. heaven,] *Q1, Q3;* heaven.
Q2.

CLYTUS.   Are you a madman? Is this a time?

LYSIMACHUS.

Yes, for I see he cannot be unjust
To me, lest something worse befall himself.

ALEXANDER.

Why dost thou tempt me thus, to thy undoing?   385
Death thou shouldst have, were it not courted so.
But know, to thy confusion, that my word,
Like destiny, admits not a reverse;
Therefore in chains thou shalt behold the nuptials
Of my Hephestion. —Guards, take him prisoner.   390

LYSIMACHUS.

I shall not easily resign my sword
Till I have dyed it in my rival's blood.

                                [Lysimachus *and guards*] *fight*.

ALEXANDER.

I charge you, kill him not. Take him alive.
The dignity of kings is now concerned,
And I will find a way to tame this beast.   395

CLYTUS.

Kneel, for I see the lightning in his eyes.

LYSIMACHUS.

I neither hope nor ask a pardon of him;
But if he should restore my sword, I would
With a new violence run against my rival.

ALEXANDER.

Sure we at last shall conquer this fierce lion.   400
Hence from my sight, and bear him to a dungeon.
Perdiccas, give this lion to a lion.
None speak for him. Fly, stop his mouth, away.

                  [*Exeunt* Perdiccas *and guards with* Lysimachus.]

CLYTUS [*aside*].

The king's extremely moved.

EUMENES [*aside*].   I dare not speak.

383–384. Yes . . . himself.]   *S-C;*   393. you,] *Q1;* you *Q2–3.*
Q1–3 divide as follows: Yes . . . me,/   396. the] *Q1; om. Q2–3.*
Lest . . . himself.   397. hope] *Q2–3;* hope, *Q1.*
392.1. *fight.*] *Q1; om. Q2–3.*

397. *hope*] expect.

CLYTUS [*aside*].

    This comes of love and women. 'Tis all madness. 405
    Yet were I heated now with wine, I should
    Be preaching to the king for this rash fool.

ALEXANDER.

    Come hither, Clytus and my dear Hephestion;
    Lend me your arms. Help, for I'm sick o'th' sudden.
    I fear betwixt Statira's cruel love 410
    And fond Roxana's arts your king will fall.

CLYTUS.

    Better the Persian race were all undone.

HEPHESTION.

    Look up, my lord, and bend not thus your head
    As you would leave the empire of the world
    Which you with toil have won.

ALEXANDER.   Would I had not, 415

    There's no true joy in such unwieldy fortune.
    Eternal gazers lasting troubles make,
    All find my spots, but few my brightness take.
    Stand off, and give me air—
    Why was I born a prince, proclaimed a god, 420
    Yet have no liberty to look abroad?
    Thus palaces in prospect bar the eye,
    Which pleased and free would o'er the cottage fly, }
    O'er flow'ry lands to the gay, distant sky.
    Farewell then, empire and the racks of love; 425
    By all the gods, I will to wilds remove,
    Stretched like a sylvan god on grass lie down,
    And quite forget that e'er I wore a crown.   [*Exeunt.*]

414. As] *Q1;* As if *Q2–3.*

---

418. *spots*] faults; with the secondary meaning of "sun-spots."
418. *take*] apprehend.
422. *in prospect*] "within the range or scope of vision" (*OED*).

ACT III

Enter Eumenes, Philip, Thessalus, Perdiccas, Lysimachus, *guards.*

EUMENES.

 Farewell, brave spirit. When you come above,
 Commend us to Philotas and the rest
 Of our great friends.

THESSALUS.   Perdiccas, you are grown

 In trust. Be thankful for your noble office.

PERDICCAS.

 As noble as you sentence me, I'd give   5
 This arm that Thessalus were so employed.

LYSIMACHUS.

 Cease these untimely jars. Farewell to all.
 Fight for the king as I have done, and then
 You may be worthy of a death like mine. —Lead on!

Enter Parisatis.

PARISATIS.

 Ah, my Lysimachus, where are you going?   10
 Whither? To be devoured? O barbarous prince!
 Could you expose your life to the king's rage,
 And yet remember mine was tied to yours?

LYSIMACHUS.

 The gods preserve you ever from the ills
 That threaten me. Live, madam, to enjoy   15
 A nobler fortune, and forget this wretch.
 I ne'er had worth, nor is it possible
 That all the blood which I shall lose this day
 Should merit this rich sorrow from your eyes.

PARISATIS.

 The king, I know, is bent to thy destruction;   20
 Now by command they forced me from his knees.
 But take this satisfaction in thy death,
 No power, command, my mother's, sister's tears,
 Shall cause me to survive thy cruel loss.

LYSIMACHUS.

 Live, princess, live! Howe'er the king disdains me,   25

---

5. *sentence*] pronounce.

Perhaps unarmed, and fighting for your sake,
I may perform what shall amaze the world,
And force him yet to give you to my arms.
Away, Perdiccas. —Dear Eumenes, take
The princess to your charge.

> *Exeunt* Perdiccas, Lysimachus, *guards.*

EUMENES.   O, cruelty!   30

PARISATIS.

Lead me, Eumenes, lead me from the light,
Where I may wait till I his ruin hear,
Then free my soul to meet him in the air.

> *Exeunt* [Parisatis *and* Eumenes].

PHILIP.

See where the jealous, proud Roxana comes;
A haughty vengeance gathers up her brow.   35

THESSALUS.

Peace, they have raised her to their ends. Observe!

> [Philip *and* Thessalus *retire.*]

> *Enter* Roxana, Cassander, Polyperchon.

ROXANA.

O, you have ruined me. I shall be mad.
Said you so passionate, is't possible?
So kind to her, and so unkind to me?

CASSANDER.

More than your utmost fancy can invent.   40
He swouned thrice at hearing of her vow,
And when our care as oft had brought back life,
He drew his sword and offered at his breast.

POLYPERCHON.

Then railed on you with such unheard-of curses.

ROXANA.

Away, begone, and give a whirlwind room,   45
Or I will blow you up like dust. Avaunt!

38. passionate] *Q1;* passionately
Q2–3.

---

36. *raised*] incited.
36.1.] Presumably Philip and Thessalus withdraw to a door on the
opposite side of the stage to watch, and leave unobtrusively later in the
scene.

Madness but meanly represents my toil.
Roxana and Statira, they are names
That must forever jar. Eternal discord,
Fury, revenge, disdain, and indignation   50
Tear my swoll'n breast, make way for fire and tempest.
My brain is burst, debate and reason quenched,
The storm is up, and my hot, bleeding heart
Splits with the rack, while passions like the winds
Rise up to heav'n and put out all the stars.   55
What saving hand, O, what almighty arm
Can raise me sinking?

CASSANDER.   Let your own arm save you.
'Tis in your power, your beauty is almighty.
Let all the stars go out, your eyes can light 'em.
Wake then, bright planet that should rule the world,   60
Wake like the moon from your too long eclipse,
And we with all the instruments of war,
Trumpets and drums, will help your glorious labor.

POLYPERCHON.

Put us to act, and with a violence
That fits the spirit of a most wronged woman.   65
Let not Medea's dreadful vengeance stand
A pattern more, but draw your own so fierce,
It may forever be original.

CASSANDER.

Touch not, but dash with strokes so bravely bold,
Till you have formed a face of so much horror   70
That gaping furies may run frighted back,
That envy may devour herself for madness,
And sad Medusa's head be turned to stone.

ROXANA.

Yes, we will have revenge, my instruments.
For there is nothing you have said of me   75
But comes far short, wanting of what I am.

---

47. *toil*] mental struggle.

54. *rack*] clouds driven by the wind.

69. *Touch*] draw or paint delicately.

73. *sad*] distressing.

73. *Medusa*] one of the three Gorgons; a female monster with snakes for hair, and a look so terrible it turned the beholder to stone.

When in my nonage I at Zogdia lived,
Amongst my she-companions I would reign;
Drew 'em from idleness and little arts
Of coining looks and laying snares for lovers;   80
Broke all their glasses and their tires tore;
Taught 'em like Amazons to ride and chase
Wild beasts in deserts, and to master men.

CASSANDER [*aside*].

Her looks, her words, her ev'ry motion fires me.

ROXANA.

But when I heard of Alexander's conquests,   85
How with a handful he had millions slain,
Spoiled all the East, their queens his captives made,
Yet with what chastity and godlike temper
He saw their beauties and with pity bowed,
Methought I hung upon my father's lips   90
And wished him tell the wondrous tale again,
Left all my sports, the woman now returned,
And sighs uncalled would from my bosom fly;
And all the night, as my Adràste told me,
In slumbers groaned, and murmured, "Alexander."   95

CASSANDER [*aside*].

Curse on the name! But I will soon remove
That bar of my ambition and my love.

ROXANA.

At last to Zogdia this triumpher came,
And, covered o'er with laurels, forced our city.
At night I by my father's order stood   100
With fifty virgins waiting at a banquet.
But, O, how glad was I to hear his court,
To feel the pressure of his glowing hand,
And taste the dear, the false-protesting lips.

CASSANDER [*aside*].

Wormwood and hemlock henceforth grow about 'em.   105

---

77. *Zogdia*] Sogdiana; province of the ancient Persian empire.
80. *coining*] artifically producing.
81. *glasses*] mirrors.
81. *tires*] clothes.
94. *Adraste*] presumably Roxana's nurse (M-J).
102. *court*] courtship.
105. *wormwood and hemlock*] plants representing bitterness and poison.

ROXANA.

 Gods! That a man should be so great and base!
 What said he not, when in the bridal bed
 He clasped my yielding body in his arms,
 When, with his fiery lips devouring mine,
 And molding with his hand my throbbing breast,   110
 He swore the globes of heav'n and earth were vile
 To those rich worlds; and talked, and kissed, and loved,
 And made me shame the morning with my blushes.

CASSANDER.

 Yet after this prove false!

POLYPERCHON.   Horrid perjury!

CASSANDER.

 Not to be matched.

POLYPERCHON.   O, you must find revenge.   115

CASSANDER.

 A person of your spirit be thus slighted,
 For whose desire all earth should be too little!

ROXANA.

 And shall the daughter of Darius hold him?
 That puny girl, that ape of my ambition,
 That cried for milk when I was nursed in blood!   120
 Shall she, made up of wat'ry element,
 A cloud, shall she embrace my proper god,
 While I am cast like lightning from his hand?
 No, I must scorn to prey on common things;
 Though hurled to earth by this disdainful Jove,   125
 I will rebound to my own orb of fire
 And with the wrack of all the heav'ns expire.

CASSANDER.

 Now you appear yourself; 'tis noble anger.

---

128. Now . . . anger.] *S-C; Q1–3* 'Tis . . . anger.
print as two lines: Now . . . yourself;/

---

 121. *made . . . element*] i.e., phlegmatic; see note above to Dryden's commendatory verses, l. 42.
 122. *proper*] own.
 126. *orb of fire*] "In some versions of the Ptolemaic system, the earth is supposed to be surrounded by a sphere of air outside of which is a sphere of fire" (M-J).
 127. *wrack*] downfall.

ROXANA.

    May the illustrious blood that fills my womb
    And ripens to be perfect godhead born,   130
    Come forth a fury, may Barsina's bastard
    Tread it to hell, and rule as sovereign lord,
    When I permit Statira to enjoy
    Roxana's right, and strive not to destroy.

       Enter Sysigambis, Statira, *in mourning.*

CASSANDER.

    Behold her going to fulfil her vow.   135
    Old Sysigambis, whom the king engaged,
    Resists and awes her with authority.

ROXANA.

    'Twas rashly vowed, indeed, and I should pity her.

SYSIGAMBIS.

    O my Statira, how has passion changed thee!
    Think, if you drive the king to such extremes,   140
    What in his fury may he not denounce
    Against the poor remains of lost Darius.

STATIRA.

    I know, I know he will be kind to you
    And to my mourning sister for my sake;
    And tell him how with my departing breath   145
    I railed not, but spoke kindly of his person,
    Nay, wept to think of our divided loves,
    And sobbing sent a last forgiveness to him.

ROXANA.

    Grant, heav'n, some ease to this distracted wretch!
    Let her not linger out a life in torments;   150
    Be these her last words, and at once dispatch her.

149. Grant,] *Q1;* Grant *Q2–3.*

---

   129. *blood . . . womb*] Roxana gave birth to a son shortly after Alexander's death.

   131. *Barsina*] Barsine, daughter of Artabazus, a Persian general, and widow of Memnon, a native of Rhodes who served under Darius. She had a son by Alexander.

   134.1.] Presumably Roxana, Cassander, and Polyperchon are standing on the opposite side of the stage. They remain unseen by Statira and Sysigambis.

   136. *engaged*] won over to his side.

SYSIGAMBIS.

 No, by the everlasting fire I swear,
 By my Darius' soul, I never more
 Will dare to look on Alexander's face,
 If you refuse to see him.   155

ROXANA.

 Curse on that cunning tongue; I fear her now.

CASSANDER.

 No, she's resolved.

STATIRA.   I cast me at your feet,
 To bathe 'em with my tears; or if you please,
 I'll let out life and wash 'em with my blood;
 But still conjure you not to rack my soul,   160
 Nor hurry my wild thoughts to perfect madness.
 Should now Darius' awful ghost appear,
 And my pale mother stand beseeching by,
 I would persist to death and keep my vow.

ROXANA.

 She shows a certain bravery of soul,   165
 Which I should praise in any but my rival.

SYSIGAMBIS.

 Die then, rebellious wretch. Thou art not now
 That soft belov'd, nor dost thou share my blood.
 Go hide thy baseness in thy lovely grot,
 Ruin thy mother and thy royal house,   170
 Pernicious creature! Shed the innocent
 Blood, and sacrifice to the king's wrath
 The lives of all thy people. Fly, begone,
 And hide thee where bright virtue never shone.
 The day will shun thee, nay, the stars that view 175
 Mischiefs and murders, deeds to thee not new,
 Will start at this. Go, go! Thy crimes deplore,
 And never think of Sysigambis more.   *Exit.*

ROXANA [*coming forward*].

 Madam, I hope you will a queen forgive.
 Roxana weeps to see Statira grieve.   180

169. lovely] *Q 1–3;* lonely *C2, S-C.*

 179.S.D. *coming forward*] Presumably Cassander and Polyperchon draw
back and leave the stage at, or shortly after, this point.

How noble is the brave resolve you make
To quit the world for Alexander's sake.
Vast is your mind, you dare thus greatly die,
And yield the king to one so mean as I.
'Tis a revenge will make the victor smart,   185
And much I fear your death will break his heart.

STATIRA.

You counterfeit a fear, and know too well
How much your eyes all beauties else excel.
Roxana, who, though not a princess born,
In chains could make the mighty victor mourn.   190
Forgetting pow'r, when wine had made him warm
And senseless, yet even then you knew to charm.
Preserve him by those arts that cannot fail,
While I the loss of what I loved bewail.

ROXANA.

I hope your majesty will give me leave   195
To wait you to the grove where you would grieve;
Where like the turtle you the loss will moan
Of that dear mate, and murmur all alone.

STATIRA.

No, proud triumpher o'er my falling state,
Thou shalt not stay to fill thee with my fate.   200
Go to the conquest which your wiles may boast,
And tell the world you left Statira lost.
Go seize my faithless Alexander's hand;
Both hand and heart were once at my command.
Grasp his loved neck, die on his fragrant breast, ⎫   205
Love him like me, which cannot be expressed, ⎬
He must be happy, and you more than blest. ⎭
While I in darkness hide me from the day, ⎫
That with my mind I may his form survey, ⎬
And think so long till I think life away. ⎭   210

ROXANA.

No, sickly virtue, no.
Thou shalt not think, nor thy love's loss bemoan,
Nor shall past pleasures through thy fancy run;

---

197. *turtle*] turtledove.
205. *die*] experience the height of passion.

That were to make thee blest as I can be.
But thy no thought I must, I will decree: 215
As thus, I'll torture thee till thou art mad,
And then no thought to purpose can be had.

STATIRA.

How frail, how cowardly is woman's mind!
We shriek at thunder, dread the rustling wind,
And glitt'ring swords the brightest eyes will blind.   220
Yet when strong jealousy enflames the soul,
The weak will roar, and calms to tempests roll.
Rival, take heed, and tempt me not too far;
My blood may boil, and blushes show a war.

ROXANA.

When you retire to your romantic cell,   225
I'll make thy solitary mansion hell;
Thou shalt not rest by day, nor sleep by night,
But still Roxana shall thy spirit fright.
Wanton, in dreams, if thou dar'st dream of bliss,
Thy roving ghost may think to steal a kiss;   230
But when to his sought bed thy wand'ring air
Shall, for the happiness it wished, repair,
How will it groan to find thy rival there!
How ghastly wilt thou look when thou shalt see,
Through the drawn curtains, that great man and me,   235
Wearied with laughing joys, shot to the soul,
While thou shalt grinning stand, and gnash thy teeth, and howl.

STATIRA.

O, barb'rous rage! My tears I cannot keep,
But my full eyes in spite of me will weep.

ROXANA.

The king and I in various pictures drawn,   240
Clasping each other, shaded o'er with lawn,
Shall be the daily presents I will send
To help thy sorrow to her journey's end.
And when we hear at last thy hour draws nigh,
My Alexander, my dear love, and I   245

---

215. *thy . . . decree*] I must and will decree that you shall not think.
231. *air*] spirit.
241. *shaded*] partially concealed, veiled.

Will come and hasten on thy ling'ring fates,
And smile and kiss thy soul out through the grates.

STATIRA.

 'Tis well, I thank thee. Thou hast waked a rage
 Whose boiling now no temper can assuage.
 I meet thy tides of jealousy with more,   250
 Dare thee to dwell, and dash thee o'er and o'er.

ROXANA.

 What would you dare?

STATIRA.   Whatever you dare do.
 My warring thoughts the bloodiest tracts pursue.
 I am by love a fury made, like you:
 Kill, or be killed; thus acted by despair.   255

ROXANA.

 Sure the disdained Statira does not dare.

STATIRA.

 Yes, tow'ring, proud Roxana, but I dare.

ROXANA.

 I tow'r indeed o'er thee;
 Like a fair wood, the shade of kings, I stand,
 While thou, sick weed, dost but infect the land. 260

STATIRA.

 No, like an ivy I will curl thee round,
 Thy sapless trunk of all its pride confound,
 Then dry and withered bend thee to the ground.
 What Sysigambis' threats, objected fears,
 My sister's sighs, and Alexander's tears   265
 Could not effect, thy rival rage has done.
 My soul, whose start at breach of oaths begun,
 Shall, to thy ruin, violated run.
 I'll see the king in spite of all I swore,
 Though curst, that thou mayst never see him more. 270

 Enter Perdiccas, Alexander, Sysigambis, *attendants, etc.*

PERDICCAS.

 Madam, your royal mother and the king.

251. dwell] *Q1–3;* duel *Q4, S-C.*   270. curst,] *Q2–3;* curst *Q1.*
260. dost] *Q1–2;* does *Q3.*

---

 251. *dwell*] stay put; but see textual note.
 255. *acted*] actuated.

ALEXANDER.

    O my Statira! O my angry dear!
    Turn thine eyes on me, I would talk to them.
    What shall I say to work upon thy soul?
    Where shall I throw me? Whither shall I fall?   275

STATIRA.

    For me you shall not fall.

ALEXANDER.   For thee I will.

    Before thy feet I'll have a grave dug up,
    And perish quick, be buried straight alive.
    Give but, as the earth grows heavy on me,
    A tender look, and a relenting word;   280
    Say but, 'twas pity that so great a man,
    Who had ten thousand deaths in battles 'scaped,
    For one poor fault so early should remove,
    And fall a martyr to the god of love.

ROXANA.

    Is then Roxana's love and life so poor   285
    That for another you can choose to die,
    Rather than live for her? What have I done?
    How am I altered since at Susa last
    You swore, and sealed it with a thousand kisses,
    Rather than lose Roxana's smallest charm,   290
    You would forego the conquest of the world?

ALEXANDER.

    Madam, you best can tell what magic drew
    Me to your charms, but let it not be told,
    For your own sake. Take, take that conquered world,
    Dispose of crowns and scepters as you please,   295
    Let me but have the freedom for an hour
    To make account with this wronged innocence.

STATIRA.

    You know, my lord, you did commit a fault.
    I ask but this: repeat your crime no more.

ALEXANDER.

    O, never, never.   300

ROXANA.

    Am I rejected then?

---

283. *remove*] depart (i.e., from this world).

ALEXANDER.   Exhaust my treasures,
    Take all the spoils of the far conquered Indies;
    But for the ease of my afflicted soul,
    Go where I never may behold thee more.

ROXANA.
    Yes, I will go, ungrateful as thou art!   305
    Bane to my life! Thou torment of my days!
    Thou murd'rer of the world! For as thy sword
    Has cut the lives of thousand thousand men,
    So will thy tongue undo all womankind.
    But I'll be gone; this last disdain has cured me,   310
    And I am now grown so indifferent,
    I could behold you kiss without a pang,
    Nay, take a torch, and light you to your bed.
    But do not trust me, no, for if you do,
    By all the furies, and the flames of love,   315
    By love, which is the hottest burning hell,
    I'll set you both on fire to blaze forever.   *Exit.*

STATIRA.
    O Alexander, is it possible? Good gods,
    That guilt can show so lovely! Yet I pardon,
    Forgive thee all, by thy dear life, I do.   320

ALEXANDER.
    Ha! Pardon! Saidst thou, pardon me?

SYSIGAMBIS.
    Now all thy mother's blessings fall about thee,
    My best, my most beloved, my own Statira.

ALEXANDER.
    Is it then true that thou hast pardoned me?
    And is it giv'n me thus to touch thy hand,   325
    And fold thy body in my longing arms?
    To gaze upon thy eyes, my happier stars?
    To taste thy lip and thy dear, balmy breath,
    While ev'ry sigh comes forth so fraught with sweets,
    'Tis incense to be offered to a god.   330

STATIRA.
    Yes, dear impostor, 'tis most true that I
    Have pardoned thee; and 'tis as true that while

310. has] *Q1;* hath *Q2–3.*   315. furies,] *Q1;* furies *Q2–3.*

I stand in view of thee, thy eyes will wound,
Thy tongue will make me wanton as thy wishes;
And while I feel thy hand, my body glows.   335
Therefore be quick, and take your last adieu,
These your last sighs, and these your parting tears.
Farewell, farewell, a long and last farewell.

ALEXANDER.

O my Hephestion, bear me, or I sink.

STATIRA.

Nay, you may take—heav'n how my heart throbs—   340
You may, you may, if yet you think me worthy,
Take from these trembling lips a parting kiss.

ALEXANDER.

No, let me starve first. Why, Statira, why?
What is the meaning of all this? O gods!
I know the cause. My working brain divines.   345
You'll say you pardoned but with this reserve,
Never to make me blest, as I have been,
To slumber by the side of that false man,
Nor give a heav'n of beauty to a devil.
Think you not thus? Speak, madam.   350

SYSIGAMBIS.

She is not worthy, son, of so much sorrow—
Speak comfort to him, speak, my dear Statira,
I ask thee by those tears. Ah, canst thou e'er
Pretend to love, yet with dry eyes behold him?

ALEXANDER.

Silence more dreadful than severest sounds.   355
Would she but speak, though death, eternal exile,
Hung at her lips, yet while her tongue pronounces,
There must be music even in my undoing.

STATIRA.

Still my loved lord, I cannot see you thus;
Nor can I ever yield to share your bed.   360
O, I shall find Roxana in your arms
And taste her kisses left upon your lips.
Her cursed embraces have defiled your body.

---

346. *pardoned . . . reserve*] only pardoned with this qualification.
354. *Pretend*] claim.

Nor shall I find the wonted sweetness there,
But artificial smells and taking odors.   365
ALEXANDER.
    Yes, obstinate, I will. Madam, you shall,
    You shall, in spite of this resistless passion,
    Be served; but you must give me leave to think
    You never loved. O, could I see you thus!
    Hell has not half the tortures that you raise.   370
CLYTUS [aside].
    Never did passions combat thus before.
ALEXANDER.
    O, I shall burst
    Unless you give me leave to rave awhile.
SYSIGAMBIS.
    Yet, ere destruction sweeps us both away,
    Relent, and break through all to pity him.   375
ALEXANDER.
    Yes, I will shake this cupid from my arms,
    If all the rages of the earth can fright him,
    Drown him in the deep bowl of Hercules,
    Make the world drunk, and then, like Aeolus,
    When he gave passage to the struggling winds,   380
    I'll strike my spear into the reeling globe
    To let it blood, set Babylon in a blaze,
    And drive this god of flames with more consuming fire.
STATIRA.
    My presence will but force him to extremes.
    Besides, 'tis death to me to see his pains,   385
    Yet stand resolved never to yield again.
    Permit me to remove.
ALEXANDER.   I charge ye, stay her;
    For if she pass, by all the hells I feel,
    Your souls, your naked ghosts, shall wait upon her.
    O, turn thee, turn! Thou barb'rous brightness, turn!   390

365. taking] *M-J*; aking *Q1–3*;   388. hells] *Q1*; hell *Q2–3*.
aching *S-C.*

---

365. *taking*] blasting, infectious; but see textual note.
375. *break through*] burst through the restraints of (i.e., of her oath).
378. *bowl of Hercules*] See I.i.245 n.
379. *Aeolus*] guardian of the winds; see *Aeneid* I. 50–101.

Hear my last words, and see my utmost pang.—
But first kneel with me, all my soldiers, kneel.   *All kneel.*
Yet lower, prostrate to the earth.—Ah, mother, what,
Will you kneel too? Then let the sun stand still
To see himself outworshipped, not a face   395
Be shown that is not washed all o'er in tears,
But weep as if you here beheld me slain.

SYSIGAMBIS.
Hast thou a heart? Or art thou savage turned?
But if this posture cannot move your mercy,
I never will speak more.

ALEXANDER.   O my Statira!   400
I swear, my queen, I'll not outlive thy hate.
My soul is still as death. But one thing more,
Pardon my last extremities, the transports
Of a deep wounded breast, and all is well.

STATIRA.
Rise, and may heav'n forgive you all, like me.   405
                                        [*All rise.*]

ALEXANDER.
You are too gracious. —Clytus, bear me hence.
When I am laid in earth, yield her the world.
There's something here heaves and is cold as ice,
That stops my breath. —Farewell, O gods, forever!

STATIRA.
Hold off, and let me run into his arms.   410
My dearest, my all love, my lord, my king,
You shall not die, if that the soul and body
Of thy Statira can restore thy life.
Give me thy wonted kindness, bend me, break me
With thy embraces.

ALEXANDER.   O, the killing joy!   415
O, ecstasy! My heart will burst my breast
To leap into thy bosom; but, by heav'n,
This night I will revenge me of thy beauties
For the dear rack I have this day endured.
For all the sighs and tears that I have spent,   420
I'll have so many thousand burning loves,

---

418. *revenge me of*] avenge myself on.

So swell thy lips, so fill me with thy sweetness,
Thou shalt not sleep, nor close thy wand'ring eyes.
The smiling hours shall all be loved away,
We'll surfeit all the night, and languish all the day.   425

STATIRA.

Nor shall Roxana—

ALEXANDER.   Let her not be named.—
O mother! How shall I requite your goodness?
And you, my fellow warriors, that could weep
For your lost king. But I invite you all,
My equals in the throne as in the grave,   430
Without distinction to the riot come,
To the king's banquet.—

CLYTUS.   I beg your majesty
Would leave me out.

ALEXANDER.   None, none shall be excused.
All revel out the day, 'tis my command. ⎱
Gay as the Persian god ourself will stand, ⎬   435
With a crowned goblet in our lifted hand. ⎰
Young Ammon and Statira shall go round, ⎱
While antic measures beat the burdened ground, ⎬
And to the vaulted skies our clangors sound. ⎰   *Exeunt.*

439. S.D. *Exeunt.*] *Q 1; om. Q 2–3.*

---

431. *riot*] extravagant feast.
435. *god*] probably Ormazd; see II.174 n.
436. *crowned*] brimming.
437. *go round*] i.e., as toasts.
438. *antic*] grotesque, bizarre.

ACT IV

[IV.i]

Enter Clytus *in his Macedonian habit;* Hephestion, Eumenes, Meleager, [*and attendants*] *in Persian robes.*

CLYTUS.

    Away, I will not wear these Persian robes;
    Nor ought the king be angry for the reverence
    I owe my country. Sacred are her customs,
    Which honest Clytus shall preserve to death.
    O, let me rot in Macedonian rags   5
    Rather than shine in fashions of the East.
    Then for the adorations he requires,
    Roast my old body in eternal flames,
    Or let him cage me like Callisthenes.

EUMENES.

    Dear Clytus, be persuaded.

HEPHESTION.   You know the king   10
    Is godlike, full of all the richest virtues
    That ever royal heart possessed; yet you,
    Perverse, but to one humor will oppose him.

CLYTUS.

    Call you it humor! 'Tis a pregnant one.
    By Mars, there's venom in it, burning pride;   15
    And though my life should follow, rather than
    Bear such a hot ambition in my bowels,
    I'd rip 'em up to give the poison vent.

MELEAGER.

    Was not that Jupiter, whom we adore,
    A man, but for his more than human acts   20
    Advanced to heav'n and worshipped for its lord!

0.2. *and attendants*] etc. *Q 1–3.*

  0.1. *habit*] attire.
  13. *humor*] whim.
  17. *bowels*] considered the seat of the emotions, especially tender emotions such as pity.
  19–21.] Lee may be referring to the legend of Zeus's secret upbringing among the shepherds of Mt. Ida, the liberation of the Cyclopes and giants, and the overthrow of the Titans.

HEPHESTION.

    By all his thunder and his sov'reign power,
    I'll not believe the earth yet ever felt
    An arm like Alexander's; not that god
    You named, though riding in a car of fire   25
    And drawn by flying horses winged with lightning,
    Could in a space more short do greater deeds,
    Drive all the nations, and lay waste the world.

CLYTUS.

    There's not a man of war amongst you all
    That loves the king like me; yet I'll not flatter   30
    Nor soothe his vanity, 'tis blamable,
    And when the wine works, Clytus' thoughts will out.

HEPHESTION.

    Then go not to the banquet.

CLYTUS.   I was called,

    My minion, was I not, as well as you?
    I'll go, my friends, in this old habit thus,   35
    And laugh, and drink the king's health heartily;
    And while you blushing bow your heads to earth,
    And hide 'em in the dust, I'll stand upright,
    Straight as a spear, the pillar of my country,
    And be by so much nearer to the gods.—   40
    But see, the king and all the court appear.

Enter Alexander, Sysigambis, Statira, Parisatis [*and attendants*].

PARISATIS.

    Spare him, O, spare Lysimachus his life.
    I know you will. Kings should delight in mercy.

ALEXANDER.

    Shield me, Statira, shield me from her sorrow.

PARISATIS.

    O, save him, save him, ere it be too late;   45
    Speak the kind word before the gaping lion
    Swallow him up. Let not your soldier perish
    But for one rashness which despair did cause.
    I'll follow thus forever on my knees,   *Kneels.*

41.1. *and attendants*] etc. *Q 1–3.*   49. S.D. *Kneels.*] *S-C; Q 1–3 assign*
                                     to l. 52.

42. *Lysimachus his*] Lysimachus's.

And make your way so slippery with tears   50
You shall not pass. —Sister, do you conjure him.

ALEXANDER.

O mother, take her, take her from me,
Her wat'ry eyes assault my very soul,
They shake my best resolve.

STATIRA.   Did not I break
Through all for you? Nay, now, my lord, you must.   55

SYSIGAMBIS.

Nor would I make my son so bold a prayer,
Had I not first consulted for his honor.

ALEXANDER.

Honor! What honor? Has not Statira said it?
Were I the king of the blue firmament,
And the bold Titans should again make war,   60
Though my resistless arrows were made ready,
By all the gods, she should arrest my hand.
Fly then, ev'n thou, his rival so beloved,
Fly with old Clytus, snatch him from the jaws
Of the devouring beast, bring him adorned   65
To the king's banquet, fit for loads of honor.

            Exeunt Hephestion, [*Clytus*,] Eumenes, Parisatis.

STATIRA.

O my loved lord! Let me embrace your knees;
I am not worthy of this mighty passion.
You are too good for goddesses themselves;
No woman, not the sex, is worth a grain   70
Of this illustrious life of my dear master.
Why are you so divine to cause such fondness
That my heart leaps, and beats, and fain would out,
To make a dance of joy about your feet?

ALEXANDER.

Excellent woman! No, 'tis impossible   75
To say how much I love thee.   [*Kisses her.*]
                    Ha! Again!
Such ecstasies life cannot carry long.

70. not] *Q 1;* nor *Q 2–3.*

----

60. *Titans*] sons and daughters of Uranus, first ruler of the world, who
were overthrown by Zeus (Jupiter).

The day comes on so fast, and beamy joy
Darts with such fierceness on me, night will follow.
A pale crowned head flew lately glaring by me   80
With two dead hands, which threw a crystal globe
From high, that shattered in a thousand pieces.
But I will lose these boding dreams in wine;
Then, warm and blushing for my queen's embraces,
Bear me with all my heat to thy loved bosom.   85

STATIRA.

Go, my best love, and cheer your drooping spirits,
Laugh with your friends, and talk your grief away,
While in the bow'r of great Semiramis
I dress your bed with all the sweets of nature,
And crown it as the altar of my love;   90
Where I will lay me down and softly mourn,
But never close my eyes till your return.

Exeunt Statira, Sysigambis.

ALEXANDER.

Is she not more than mortal man can wish!
Diana's soul cast in the flesh of Venus!
By Jove, 'tis ominous, our parting is.   95
Her face looked pale, too, as she turned away;
And when I wrung her by the rosy fingers,
Methought the strings of my great heart did crack.
What should it mean? —Forward, Laomedon!

Roxana *meets him, with* Cassander, Polyperchon, Philip *and* Thessalus.

Why, madam, gaze you thus?

ROXANA.   For a last look,   100

She holds his hand.

And that the memory of Roxana's wrongs
May be forever printed in your mind.

ALEXANDER.

O madam, you must let me pass.

ROXANA.   I will;
But I have sworn that you shall hear me speak,
And mark me well, for fate is in my breath.   105
Love on the mistress you adore to death.

---

99. *Laomedon*] historically one of Alexander's generals.

Still hope, but I fruition will destroy.
Languish for pleasures you shall ne'er enjoy.
Still may Statira's image draw your sight,
Like those deluding fires that walk at night,   110
Lead you through fragrant grots and flow'ry groves,
And charm you through deep grass with sleeping loves,
That when your fancy to its height does rise, ⎱
The light you loved may vanish from your eyes, ⎰
Darkness, despair, and death your wand'ring soul surprise.⎰ 115

ALEXANDER.

    Away! Lead, Meleager, to the banquet.

                              Exit [*with* Meleager, *and attendants*].

ROXANA.

    So unconcerned! O, I could tear my flesh,
    Or him, or you, nay, all the world, to pieces.

CASSANDER.

    Still keep this spirit up, preserve it still,
    Lose not a grain, for such majestic atoms   120
    First made the world, and must preserve its greatness.

ROXANA.

    I know I am whatever thou canst say.
    My soul is pent, and has not elbow room;
    'Tis swelled with this last slight beyond all bounds.
    O, that it had a space might answer to   125
    Its infinite desire, where I might stand
    And hurl the spheres about like sportive balls.

CASSANDER.

    We are your slaves, admirers of your fury.
    Command Cassander to obey your pleasure,
    And I will on, swift as my nimble eye   130
    Scales heav'n when I am angry with the fates.
    No age, nor sex, nor dignity of blood,
    No ties of law or nature, not the life
    Imperial, though guarded with the gods,
    Shall bar Cassander's vengeance. He shall die.   135

116.1. *Exit*] *Ex. cum suis. Q 1–3.*   133. or] *Q 1;* nor *Q 2–3.*

124. *pent*] "distended or strained by being overfull of something" (*OED*).
127. *sportive*] used in sport. (The earliest instance of this usage recorded in *OED* is 1705.)

ROXANA.

    Ha! Shall he die? Shall I consent to kill him?
    To see him clasped in the cold arms of death,
    Whom I with such an eagerness have loved?
    Do I not bear his image in my womb?
    Which, while I meditate and roll revenge,   140
    Starts in my body like a fatal pulse,
    And strikes compassion through my bleeding bowels.

POLYPERCHON.

    These scruples which your love would raise might pass,
    Were not the empire of the world considered.
    How will the glorious infant in your womb,   145
    When time shall teach his tongue, be bound to curse you,
    If now you strike not for his coronation!

CASSANDER.

    If Alexander lives, you cannot reign,
    Nor shall your child. Old Sysigambis' head
    Will not be idle. Sure destruction waits   150
    Both you and yours. Let not your anger cool,
    But give the word. Say, "Alexander bleeds!
    Draw dry the veins of all the Persian race,
    And hurl a ruin o'er the East!"—'tis done.

POLYPERCHON.

    Behold the instruments of this great work.   155

PHILIP.

    Behold your forward slave.

THESSALUS.   I'll execute.

ROXANA.

    And when this ruin is accomplished, where
    Shall curst Roxana fly with this dear load?
    Where shall she find a refuge from the arms
    Of all the successors of this great man?   160
    No barb'rous nation will receive a guilt
    So much transcending theirs, but drive me out.
    The wildest beasts will hunt me from their dens,
    And birds of prey molest me in the grave.

140. meditate] meditate, *Q1–3*.   147. his] *Q1;* om. *Q2–3.*

140. *meditate*] "plan by revolving in the mind" (*OED*).
152–154. *Say . . . done*] i.e., only give this command, and the deed is as good as done.

CASSANDER.

    No, you shall live. Pardon the insolence   165
    Which this almighty love enforces from me,
    You shall live safer, nobler than before
    In your Cassander's arms.

ROXANA.

    Disgraced Roxana, whither wilt thou fall!
    I ne'er was truly wretched till this moment;   170
    There's not one mark of former majesty
    To awe my slave that offers at my honor.

CASSANDER.

    Madam, I hope you'll not impute my passion
    To want of that respect which I must bear you.
    Long I have loved—

ROXANA.   Peace, most audacious villain!   175
    Or I will stab this passion in thy throat.
    What, shall I leave the bosom of a deity
    To clasp a clod, a moving piece of earth,
    Which a mole heaves? So far art thou beneath me.

CASSANDER.

    Your majesty shall hear no more my folly.   180

ROXANA.

    Nor dare to meet my eyes; for if thou dost,
    With a love-glance thy plots are all unravelled,
    And your kind thoughts of Alexander told,
    Whose life, in spite of all his wrongs to me,
    Shall be forever sacred and untouched.   185

CASSANDER.

    I know, dread madam, that Cassander's life
    Is in your hands so cast to do you service.

ROXANA.

    You thought, perhaps, because I practiced charms
    To gain the king, that I had loose desires.
    No, 'tis my pride that gives me height of pleasure.   190
    To see the man by all the world admired,
    Bowed to my bosom and my captive there.
    Then my veins swell and my arms grasp the poles,

187. hands] *Q1;* hands, *Q2–3.*

172. *offers at*] makes an attempt upon.

My breasts grow bigger with the vast delight,
'Tis length of rapture and an age of fury.   195

CASSANDER.

By your own life, the greatest oath I swear,
Cassander's passion from this time is dumb.

ROXANA.

No, if I were a wanton, I would make
Princes the victims of my raging fires.
I, like the changing moon, would have the stars   200
My followers, and mantled kings by night
Should wait my call; fine slaves to quench my flame,
Who, lest in dreams they should reveal the deed,
Still as they came, successively should bleed.

CASSANDER [kneeling].

To make atonement for the highest crime,   205
I beg your majesty will take the life
Of Queen Statira as a sacrifice.

ROXANA.

Rise, thou hast made me ample expiation.
Yes, yes, Statira, rival, thou must die;
I know this night is destined for my ruin,   210
And Alexander from the glorious revels
Flies to thy arms.

PHILIP.

The bowers of Semiramis are made
The scene this night of their new-kindled loves.

ROXANA.

Methinks I see her yonder, O, the torment!   215
Busy for bliss and full of expectation.
She adorns her head, and her eyes give new luster,
Languishes in her glass, tries all her looks,
Steps to the door and listens for his coming,
Runs to the bed, and kneels, and weeps, and wishes,   220
Then lays the pillow easy for his head,
Warms it with sighs, and molds it with her kisses.
O, I am lost, torn with imagination!
Kill me, Cassander, kill me instantly,
That I may haunt her with a thousand devils.   225

CASSANDER.

Why d'ye stop to end her while you may?

No time so proper as the present now.
While Alexander feasts with all his court,
Give me your eunuchs, half your Zogdian slaves,
I'll do the deed; nor shall a waiter 'scape,   230
That serves your rival, to relate the news.

POLYPERCHON.

She was committed to Eumenes' charge.

ROXANA.

Eumenes dies, and all that are about her.
Nor shall I need your aid; you'll love again.
I'll head the slaves myself with this drawn dagger,   235
To carry death that's worthy of a queen.
A common fate ne'er rushes from my hand,
'Tis more than life to die by my command.
And when she sees
That to my arm her ruin she must owe,   ⎫   240
Her thankful head will straight be bended low, ⎬
Her heart shall leap half way to meet the blow. ⎭

Exit Roxana.

CASSANDER.

Go thy ways, Semele. —She scorns to sin
Beneath a god. We must be swift. The ruin
We intend, who knows, she may discover.   245

POLYPERCHON.

It must be acted suddenly. Tonight
Now at the banquet Philip holds his cup.

PHILIP.

And dares to execute. Propose his fate.

CASSANDER.

Observe in this small vial certain death;
It holds a poison of such deadly force,   250
Should Aesculapius drink it, in five hours

246. suddenly. Tonight] suddenly,   *Q2–3.*
tonight *Q1;* suddenly, tonight,

---

230. *waiter*] attendant.
243. *Semele*] daughter of Cadmus of Thebes. Jupiter, disguised as a
mortal, had a love affair with her, but Juno incited her to make him reveal
himself in all his glory, knowing that Semele would then be consumed in
thunder and lightning.
246. *suddenly*] without delay.
251. *Aesculapius*] god of medicine.

(For then it works) the god himself were mortal.
I drew it from Nonarris' horrid spring.
A drop infused in wine will seal his death,
And send him howling to the lowest shades.   255
PHILIP.
    Would it were done.
CASSANDER.   O, we shall have him tear,
    Ere yet the moon has half her journey rode,
    The world to atoms; for it scatters pains
    All sorts, and through all nerves, veins, arteries,
    Even with extremity of frost it burns,   260
    Drives the distracted soul about her house,
    Which runs to all the pores, the doors of life,
    Till she is forced for air to leave her dwelling.
POLYPERCHON.
    By Pluto's self, the work is wondrous brave.
CASSANDER.
    Now separate. Philip and Thessalus,   265
    Haste to the banquet. At his second call
    Give him the fatal draught that crowns the night,
    While Polyperchon and myself retire.
                     Exeunt omnes praeter Cassander.
    Yes, Alexander, now thou payst me well;
    Blood for a blow is interest indeed.   270
    Methinks I am grown taller with the murder,
    And standing straight on this majestic pile
    I hit the clouds and see the world below me.
    O, 'tis the worst of racks to a brave spirit
    To be born base, a vassal, a curst slave.   275
    Now, by the project lab'ring in my brain,
    'Tis nobler far to be the king of hell,
    To head infernal legions, chiefs below,
    To let 'em loose for earth, to call 'em in
    And take account of what dark deeds are done,   280

---

253. *Nonarris*] Nonacris; city in Arcadia, where the river Styx took its origin. Its waters were believed to be poisonous.
  264. *Pluto*] god of the underworld.
  268.1. *praeter*] except.
  277–282.] Lee may here have been indebted to Milton's *Paradise Lost*, I. 263.

Than be a subject-god in heav'n unblest,
And without mischief have eternal rest.   *Exit.*

[IV.ii]

The scene draws. Alexander *is seen standing on a throne with all his commanders about him holding goblets in their hands.*

ALEXANDER.
          To our immortal health, and our fair queen's.
          All drink it deep, and while it flies about,
          Mars and Bellona join to make us music.
          A hundred bulls be offered to the sun,
          White as his beams. Speak the big voice of war,   5
          Beat all our drums, and blow our silver trumpets,
          Till we provoke the gods to act our pleasure
          In bowls of nectar and replying thunder.
                    [*Drums and trumpets*] *sound while they drink.*

Enter Hephestion, Clytus, *leading in* Lysimachus *in his shirt, bloody,*
Perdiccas, *guard.*

CLYTUS.
          Long live the king, and conquest crown his arms
          With laurels ever green. Fortune's his slave,   10
          And kisses all that fight upon his side.

ALEXANDER.
          Did I not give command you should preserve
          Lysimachus?

HEPHESTION.
          You did.

ALEXANDER.   What then portend those bloody marks?

HEPHESTION.
          Your mercy flew too late. Perdiccas had,   15
          According to the dreadful charge you gave,
          Already placed the prince in a lone court,
          Unarmed, all but his hands, on which he wore
          A pair of gauntlets; such was his desire,

1. queen's] *Q2–3;* queens *Q1.*   *after l. 7.*
8.1. *sound . . . drink.*] *Q2–3; in Q1*   12. I not] *Q1;* not I *Q2–3.*

3. *Bellona*] goddess of war.

To show in death the difference betwixt   20
The blood of the Aeacides and common men.

CLYTUS.

At last the door of an old lion's den
Being drawn up, the horrid beast appeared.
The flames, which from his eyes shot gloomy red,
Made the sun start, as the spectators thought,   25
And round 'em cast a day of blood and death.

HEPHESTION.

When we arrived, just as the valiant prince
Cried out, "O Parisatis, take my life.
'Tis for thy sake I go undaunted thus
To be devoured by this most dreadful creature."   30

CLYTUS.

Then walking forward, the large beast descried
His prey, and with a roar that made us pale,
Flew fiercely on him; but the active prince,
Starting aside, avoided his first shock
With a slight hurt, and, as the lion turned,   35
Thrust gauntlet, arm and all, into his throat,
And with Herculean force tore forth by th' roots
The foaming, bloody tongue; and while the savage,
Faint with that loss, sunk to the blushing earth
To plough it with his teeth, your conqu'ring soldier   40
Leaped on his back and dashed his skull to pieces.

ALEXANDER.

By all my laurels, 'twas a godlike act,
And 'tis my glory, as it shall be thine,
That Alexander could not pardon thee.
O my brave soldier! Think not all the prayers   45
Of the lamenting queens could move my soul
Like what thou hast performed. Grow to my breast.
                                        Embraces him.

LYSIMACHUS.

However love did hurry my wild arm,
When I was cool, my fev'rish blood did bate,
And as I went to death, I blessed the king.   50

---

21. *Aeacides*] descendants of Aeacus, son of Zeus and Aegina, grand-
father of Achilles.
49. *bate*] "fall off in force or intensity" (*OED*).

ALEXANDER.

    Lysimachus, we both have been transported,
    But from this hour be certain of my heart.
    A lion be the impress of thy shield,
    And that gold armor we from Porus won
    The king presents thee. But retire to bed;   55
    Thy toils ask rest.

LYSIMACHUS.   I have no wounds to hinder
    Of any moment; or if I had, though mortal,
    I'd stand to Alexander's health till all
    My veins were dry, and fill 'em up again
    With that rich blood which makes the gods immortal.   60

ALEXANDER.

    Hephestion, thy hand. Embrace him close.
    Though next my heart you hang, the jewel there,
    For scarce I know whether my queen be dearer,
    Thou shalt not rob me of my glory, youth,
    That must to ages flourish. Parisatis   65
    Shall now be his that serves me best in war.
    Neither reply, but mark the charge I give,
    And live as friends. —Sound, sound my army's honor.
    Health to their bodies, and eternal fame
    Wait on their memory, when those are ashes.   70
    Live all, you must: 'tis a god gives you life.

[Drums and trumpets] sound. [All drink.] Lysimachus *offers* Clytus *a Persion robe and he refuses it.*

CLYTUS.

    O, vanity!

ALEXANDER.   Ha! What says Clytus?
    Who am I?

CLYTUS.   The son of good King Philip.

54. gold] *Q1;* golden *Q2–3.*   62. hang,] hang *Q1–3.*
54. Porus] *C3;* Porcus *Q1–3.*   68. army's] armies *Q1–3.*
61. hand.] hand, *Q1;* hand *Q2–3.*   71. all,] all *Q1–3.*

---

53. *impress*] impresa; heraldic device.
54. *Porus*] Indian king who fought a long battle to prevent Alexander crossing the river Hydaspes in 327 B.C.
56. *hinder*] "delay or frustrate action" (*OED*).
69.] Presumably at this point Philip hands Alexander the poisoned goblet; see IV.i.266–267.

ALEXANDER.

No, 'tis false.
By all my kindred in the skies,   75
Jove made my mother pregnant.

CLYTUS.   I ha' done.

Here follows an entertainment of Indian singers and dancers.

The music flourishes.

ALEXANDER.

Hold, hold! Clytus, take the robe.

CLYTUS.   Sir, the wine.
The weather's hot; besides, you know my humor.

ALEXANDER.

O, 'tis not well. I'd burn rather than be
So singular and froward.

CLYTUS.   So would I   80
Burn, hang, or drown; but in a better cause
I'll drink or fight for sacred majesty
With any here. —Fill me another bowl.—
Will you excuse me?

ALEXANDER.   You will be excused.
But let him have his humor; he is old.   85

CLYTUS.

So was your father, sir. This to his memory.
Sound all the trumpets there.

ALEXANDER.   They shall not sound
Till the king drinks. By Mars, I cannot taste
A moment's rest for all my years of blood
But one or other will oppose my pleasure.   90
Sure I was formed for war, eternal war;
All, all are Alexander's enemies,
Which I could tame. Yes, the rebellious world
Should feel my wrath. —But let the sports go on.

The Indians dance.

LYSIMACHUS.

Nay, Clytus, you that could advise—

77. hold!] hold; *C2;* hold, *Q1–3.*   88. taste] *Q1;* take *Q2–3.*

76.2. *music*] band of musicians.   76.2. *flourishes*] sounds a fanfare.
80. *singular*] "differing from others in opinion; standing alone" (*OED*).
80. *froward*] perverse.

ALEXANDER.   Forbear!   95
    Let him persist, be positive and proud,
    Sullen and dazzled amongst the nobler souls,
    Like an infernal spirit that had stole
    From hell and mingled with the laughing gods.

CLYTUS.
    When gods grow hot, where is the difference   100
    'Twixt them and devils? —Fill me Greek wine, yet fuller,
    For I want spirits.

ALEXANDER.   Ha! Let me hear a song.

CLYTUS.
    Music for boys. Clytus would hear the groans
    Of dying persons and the horses' neighings;
    Or if I must be tortured with shrill voices,   105
    Give me the cries of matrons in sacked towns.

HEPHESTION.
    Lysimachus, the king looks sad. Let us awake him.
    Health to the son of Jupiter Ammon.
    Ev'ry man take his goblet in his hand,
    Kneel all, and kiss the earth with adoration.   110

ALEXANDER.
    Sound, sound, that all the universe may hear.
    That I could speak like Jove, to tell abroad
    The kindness of my people. —Rise, O, rise!
    My hands, my arms, my heart is ever yours.

         Comes from his throne. All kiss his hand.

CLYTUS.
    I did not kiss the earth, nor must your hand;   115
    I am unworthy, sir.

ALEXANDER.   I know thou art.
    Thou enviest my great honor. —Sit, my friends.
    Nay, I must have a room. —Now let us talk
    Of war, for what more fits a soldier's mouth?
    And speak, speak freely, or ye do not love me,   120
    Who think you was the bravest general
    That ever led an army to the field?

100. where is] *Q1;* where's *Q2–3.*   118. a] *Q1; om. Q2–3.*

118. *room*] place.

HEPHESTION.

> I think the sun himself ne'er saw a chief
> So truly great, so fortunately brave,
> As Alexander; not the famed Alcides, 125
> Nor fierce Achilles, who did twice destroy
> With their all-conqu'ring arms the famous Troy.

LYSIMACHUS.

> Such was not Cyrus.

ALEXANDER. O, you flatter me.

CLYTUS.

> They do indeed, and yet you love 'em for it,
> But hate old Clytus for his hardy virtue. 130
> Come, shall I speak a man more brave than you,
> A better general and more expert soldier?

ALEXANDER.

> I should be glad to learn. Instruct me, sir.

CLYTUS.

> Your father, Philip. I have seen him march,
> And fought beneath his dreadful banner, where 135
> The stoutest at this table would ha' trembled.
> Nay, frown not, sir; you cannot look me dead.
> When Greeks joined Greeks, then was the tug of war,
> The labored battle sweat, and conquest bled.
> Why should I fear to speak a truth more noble 140
> Than e'er your father Jupiter Ammon told you:
> Philip fought men, but Alexander women.

ALEXANDER.

> Spite, by the gods, proud spite, and burning envy!
> Is then my glory come to this at last,
> To vanquish women? Nay, he said the stoutest here 145
> Would tremble at the dangers he has seen.
> In all the sicknesses and wounds I bore,
> When from my reins the javelin's head was cut,
> Lysimachus, Hephestion, speak, Perdiccas,

---

125. *Alcides*] Hercules sacked Troy after being cheated by King Laomedon.
128. *Cyrus*] founder of the Persian empire in the sixth century B.C.
138. *tug of war*] "the decisive contest; the real struggle or tussle" (*OED*).
139. *labored*] hard-worked.
148. *reins*] loins (strictly, the kidneys).

Did I tremble? O, the cursed liar!   150
Did I once shake or groan, or bear myself
Beneath my majesty, my dauntless courage?

HEPHESTION.

Wine has transported him.

ALEXANDER.   No, 'tis plain, mere malice.—
I was a woman too at Oxydrace,
When, planting at the walls a scaling-ladder,   155
I mounted spite of show'rs of stones, bars, arrows,
And all the lumber which they thundered down,
When you beneath cried out, and spread your arms,
That I should leap amongst you. Did I so?

LYSIMACHUS.

Turn the discourse, my lord; the old man raved.   160

ALEXANDER.

Was I a woman when like Mercury
I left the walls to fly amongst my foes,
And like a baited lion dyed myself
All over with the blood of those bold hunters?
Till, spent with toil, I battled on my knees,   165
Plucked forth the darts that made my shield a forest,
And hurled 'em back with most unconquered fury.

CLYTUS.

'Twas all bravado, for before you leapt,
You saw that I had burst the gates in sunder.

ALEXANDER.

Did I then turn me like a coward round   170
To seek for succor? Age cannot be so base.
That thou wert young again. I would put off
My majesty to be more terrible,
That like an eagle I might strike this hare
Trembling to earth, shake thee to dust, and tear   175
Thy heart for this bold lie, thou feeble dotard.

He tosses fruit at him as they rise.

176.1. *He . . . rise.*] *S-C; in Q1–3
after l. 177.*

153. *plain*] downright.
154. *Oxydrace*] Indian city which put up fierce resistance to Alexander in
327 B.C.

CLYTUS.

What, do you pelt me, like a boy, with apples?
Kill me, and bury the disgrace I feel.
I know the reason that you use me so,
Because I saved your life at Grannicus,   180
And, when your back was turned, opposed my breast
To bold Rhesaces' sword; you hate me for't,
You do, proud prince.

ALEXANDER.   Away, your breath's too hot.

Flings from him.

CLYTUS.

You hate the benefactor, though you took
The gift, your life, from this dishonored Clytus,   185
Which is the blackest, worst ingratitude.

ALEXANDER.

Go, leave the banquet. Thus far I forgive thee.

CLYTUS.

Forgive yourself for all your blasphemies,
The riots of a most debauched and blotted life,
Philotas' murder—

ALEXANDER.   Ha! What said the traitor?   190

LYSIMACHUS.

Eumenes, let us force him hence.

CLYTUS.   Away!

HEPHESTION.

You shall not tarry. Drag him to the door.

CLYTUS.

No, let him send me, if I must be gone,
To Philip, Attalus, Callisthenes,
To great Parmenio and his slaughtered sons: 195
Parmenio, who did many brave exploits
Without the king, the king without him nothing.

ALEXANDER.

Give me a javelin.   *Takes one from the guards.*

HEPHESTION.   Hold, sir.

192. You . . . door.] *S-C; Q 1–3*   Drag . . . door.
print as two lines: You . . . tarry;/   195. and] *Q 1;* and to *Q 2–3.*

189. *blotted*] tarnished.
194. *Attalus*] uncle of Cleopatra, Philip's second wife. He insulted
Alexander, who later had him murdered.

ALEXANDER.   Off, sirrah, lest
    At once I strike it through his heart and thine.

LYSIMACHUS.
    O sacred sir, have but a moment's patience.   200

ALEXANDER.
    Preach patience to another lion. —What,
    Hold my arms? I shall be murdered here,
    Like poor Darius, by my own barb'rous subjects.
    Perdiccas, sound my trumpets to the camp,
    Call all my soldiers to the court; nay, haste,   205
    For there is treason plotting 'gainst my life,
    And I shall perish ere they come to rescue.

LYSIMACHUS, HEPHESTION.
    Let us all die, ere think so damned a deed.   *[They] kneel.*

ALEXANDER.
    Where is the traitor?

CLYTUS.   Sure there's none about you;
    But here stands honest Clytus, whom the king   210
    Invited to his banquet.

ALEXANDER.
    Begone, and sup with Philip,   *Strikes him through.*
    Parmenio, Attalus, Callisthenes,
    And let bold subjects learn by thy sad fate,
    To tempt the patience of a man above 'em.   215

CLYTUS.
    The rage of wine is drowned in gushing blood.
    O Alexander, I have been too blame.
    Hate me not after death, for I repent
    That so I urged your noblest, sweetest nature.

ALEXANDER.
    What's this I hear? Say on, my dying soldier.   220

CLYTUS.
    I should ha' killed myself, had I but lived
    To be once sober. Now I fall with honor.
    My own hand would ha' brought foul death. O, pardon.

                                                     Dies.

208. Let us] *Q1;* Let's *Q2–3.*   217. too] *Q1;* to *Q2–3.*

202–203. *murdered . . . subjects*] Darius was murdered by Bessus, satrap of Bactria, and his followers in 330 B.C.

    217. *too blame*] "In the 16th–17th c. the *to* was misunderstood as *too,* and blame taken as adj. = blameworthy, culpable" (*OED*).

ALEXANDER.

    Then I am lost. What has my vengeance done?
    Who is it thou hast slain? Clytus; what was he?   225
    Thy faithful subject, worthiest counselor,
    Who for the saving of thy life has now
    A noble recompense; for one rash word,
    For a forgetfulness which wine did work,
    The poor, the honest Clytus thou hast slain!   230
    Are these the laws of hospitality?
    Thy friends will shun thee now, and stand at distance,
    Nor dare to speak their minds, nor eat with thee,
    Nor drink, lest by thy madness they die too.

HEPHESTION.

    Guards, take the body hence.

ALEXANDER.   None dare to touch him,   235
    For we must never part. Cruel Hephestion,
    And you, Lysimachus, that had the power,
    Yet would not hold me.

LYSIMACHUS.   Dear sir, we did.

ALEXANDER.   I know it;
    Ye held me like a beast, to let me go
    With greater violence. O, you have undone me!   240
    Excuse it not, you that could stop a lion,
    Could not turn me. You should have drawn your swords
    And barred my rage with their advancing points,
    Made reason glitter in my dazzled eyes
    Till I had seen what ruin did attend me.   245
    That had been noble, that had showed a friend.
    Clytus would so have done to save your lives.

LYSIMACHUS.

    When men shall hear how highly you were urged—

ALEXANDER.

    No, you have let me stain my rising virtue,
    Which else had ended brighter than the sun.   250
    Death, hell, and furies! You have sunk my glory.
    O, I am all a blot, which seas of tears
    And my heart's blood can never wash away;

227–229. Who . . . work,] *Q1;* Who   Granike,/ Has now a noble recom-
for saving of thy life, when/ Thou   pence; for speaking rashly, *Q2–3.*
fought'st bare-headed at the river   237. you] *Q1; om. Q2–3.*

246. *had . . . friend*] would have shown the behavior of a true friend.

    Yet 'tis but just I try, and on the point
    Still reeking hurl my black, polluted breast.   255

HEPHESTION.

    O sacred sir, this must not be.

EUMENES.

    Forgive my pious hands.

LYSIMACHUS.

    And mine, that dare disarm my master.

ALEXANDER.

    Yes, cruel men, you now can show your strength;
    Here's not a slave but dares oppose my justice.   260
    Yet I will render all endeavors vain
    That tend to save my life.—   *Falls.*
                 Here I will lie
    Close to his bleeding side, thus kissing him,
    These pale dead lips that have so oft advised me,
    Thus bathing o'er his reverend face in tears,   265
    Thus clasping his cold body in my arms,
    Till death, like him, has made me stiff and horrid.

HEPHESTION.

    What shall we do?

LYSIMACHUS.   I know not. My wounds bleed afresh
    With striving with him. Perdiccas, lend's your arm.
                  Exit Perdiccas, Lysimachus.

HEPHESTION.

    Call Aristander hither,   270
    Or Meleager. Let's force him from the body.

    Cries without: "*Arm, arm! Treason, treason!*" *Enter* Perdiccas *bloody.*

PERDICCAS.

    Haste, all take arms! Hephestion, where's the king?

HEPHESTION.

    There, by old Clytus' side, whom he has slain.

259. you] *Q1;* ye *Q2–3.*

    271.1. *Enter Perdiccas*] Stroup and Cooke (S-C, I, 472) point out that Perdiccas has only just left the stage, yet now speaks and is addressed as if he had been attending Statira elsewhere. They suggest that Eumenes would make a more appropriate messenger, and IV.i.232–233 confirm that he was Lee's original choice. However, Eumenes is already on stage (see l. 257 above). Kemble's solution was to have Perdiccas leave at l. 207.

PERDICCAS.

    Then misery on misery will fall,
    Like rolling billows to advance the storm.   275
    Rise, sacred sir, and haste to aid the queen;
    Roxana, filled with furious jealousy,
    Came with a guard of Zogdian slaves unmarked,
    And broke upon me with such sudden rage
    That all are perished who resistance made.   280
    I only with these wounds through clashing spears
    Have forced my way to give you timely notice.

ALEXANDER.

    What says Perdiccas? Is the queen in danger?

PERDICCAS.

    She dies unless you turn her fate, and quickly;
    Your distance from the palace asks more speed,   285
    And the ascent to th' flying grove is high.

ALEXANDER.

    Thus from the grave I rise to save my love.
    All draw your swords, with wings of lightning move.
    When I rush on, sure none will dare to stay;
    'Tis beauty calls, and glory shows the way.   *Exeunt.* 290

---

286. *flying grove*] i.e., the hanging gardens.

ACT V

Statira *is discovered sleeping in the Bower of Semiramis. The spirits of* Queen Statira, *her mother, and* Darius *appear standing on each side of her with daggers, threatening her. They sing.*

DARIUS.

    Is innocence so void of cares
    That it can undisturbed sleep
    Amidst the noise of horrid wars
    That make immortal spirits weep?

QUEEN STATIRA.

    No boding crows nor ravens come   5
    To warn her of approaching doom?

DARIUS.

    She walks, as she dreams, in a garden of flowers,
    And her hands are employed in the beautiful bowers.
    She dreams of the man that is far from the grove,
    And all her soft fancy still runs on her love.   10

QUEEN STATIRA.

    She nods o'er the brooks that run purling along,
    And the nightingales lull her more fast with a song.

DARIUS.

    But see the sad end which the gods have decreed.

QUEEN STATIRA.

    This poniard's thy fate.

DARIUS.   My daughter must bleed.

CHORUS.

    Awake then, Statira, awake, for alas you must die.   15
    Ere an hour be past, you must breathe out your last.

DARIUS.

    And be such another as I.

QUEEN STATIRA.

    As I.

CHORUS.

    And be such another as I.   [*Exeunt* Spirits.]

---

12. *fast*] sound (asleep).
15. S.P. *Chorus*] i.e., both together.

Statira *sola.*

STATIRA.

Bless me, ye pow'rs above, and guard my virtue!   20
I saw, nor was't a dream, I saw and heard
My royal parents; there I saw 'em stand.
My eyes beheld their precious images;
I heard their heav'nly voices. Where, O, where
Fled you so fast, dear shades, from my embraces.   25
You told me this: this hour should be my last,
And I must bleed. —Away, 'tis all delusion!
Do not I wait for Alexander's coming?
None but my loving lord can enter here;
And will he kill me? Hence, fantastic shadows!   30
And yet methinks he should not stay thus long.
Why do I tremble thus? If I but stir,
The motion of my robes makes my heart leap.
When will the dear man come, that all my doubts
May vanish in his breast? that I may hold him   35
Fast as my fears can make me, hug him close
As my fond soul can wish, give all my breath
In sighs and kisses, swoun, die away with rapture!
But hark, I hear him—   *Noise within.*
     Fain I would hide my blushes.
I hear his tread, but dare not go to meet him.   40

   Enter Roxana *with slaves and a dagger.*

ROXANA.

At length we have conquered this stupendious height,
These flying groves, whose wonderful ascent
Leads to the clouds.

STATIRA.   Then all the vision's true,   *Retires.*
And I must die, lose my dear lord forever.
That, that's the murder.

ROXANA.   Shut the brazen gate,   45
And make it fast with all the massy bars.
I know the king will fly to her relief,
But we have time enough. —Where is my rival?

45. murder] *Q1–2;* murderer *Q3.*

_____

19.1. *sola*] alone.
30. *fantastic*] imaginary.

Appear, Statira, now no more a queen,
Roxana calls. Where is your majesty?   50

STATIRA [*coming forward*].

And what is she who with such tow'ring pride
Would awe a princess that is born above her?

ROXANA.

I like the port imperial beauty bears;
It shows thou hast a spirit fit to fall
A sacrifice to fierce Roxana's wrongs.   55
Be sudden then, put forth these royal breasts,
Where our false master has so often languished,
That I may change their milky innocence
To blood, and dye me in a deep revenge.

STATIRA.

No, barb'rous woman! Though I durst meet death   60
As boldly as our lord, with a resolve
At which thy coward heart would tremble,
Yet I disdain to stand the fate you offer,
And therefore, fearless of thy dreadful threats,
Walk thus regardless by thee.

ROXANA.   Ha! So stately!   65
This sure will sink you.

STATIRA.   No, Roxana, no.
The blow you give will strike me to the stars,
But sink my murd'ress in eternal ruin.

ROXANA.

Who told you this?

STATIRA.   A thousand spirits tell me.
There's not a god but whispers in my ear   70
This death will crown me with immortal glory;
To die so fair, so innocent, so young,
Will make me company for queens above.

ROXANA.

Preach on.

STATIRA.   While you, the burden of the earth,
Fall to the deep so heavy with thy guilt   75
That hell itself must groan at thy reception;

---

53. *port*] deportment, bearing.
56. *sudden*] quick to act.

While foulest fiends shun thy society,
And thou shalt walk alone, forsaken fury.

ROXANA.

    Heav'n witness for me, I would spare thy life
    If anything but Alexander's love   80
    Were in debate. Come, give me back his heart,
    And thou shalt live, live empress of the world.

STATIRA.

    The world is less than Alexander's love,
    Yet, could I give it, 'tis not in my power.
    This I dare promise, if you spare my life,   85
    Which I disdain to beg, he shall speak kindly.

ROXANA.

    Speak! Is that all?

STATIRA.   Perhaps at my request,
    And for a gift so noble as my life,
    Bestow a kiss.

ROXANA.   A kiss! No more?

STATIRA [*aside*].   O gods!
    What shall I say to work her to my end?   90
    Fain I would see him. —[*Aloud.*]   Yes, a little more,
    Embrace you, and forever be your friend.

ROXANA.

    O, the provoking word! Your friend! Thou di'st.
    Your friend! What, must I bring you then together?
    Adorn your bed and see you softly laid?   95
    By all my pangs, and labors of my love,
    This has thrown off all that was sweet and gentle;
    Therefore—

STATIRA.   Yet hold thy hand advanced in air.
    I see my death is written in thy eyes,
    Therefore wreak all thy lust of vengeance on me,   100
    Wash in my blood, and steep thee in my gore,
    Feed like a vulture, tear my bleeding heart.
    But O Roxana! That there may appear
    A glimpse of justice for thy cruelty,
    A grain of goodness for a mass of evil,   105
    Give me my death in Alexander's presence.

ROXANA.

    Not for the rule of heav'n. Are you so cunning?

What, you would have him mourn you as you fall?
Take your farewell, and taste such healing kisses
As might call back your soul? No, thou shalt fall   110
Now, and when death has seized thy beauteous limbs,
I'll have thy body thrown into a well,
Buried beneath a heap of stones forever.

Enter a Slave.

SLAVE.

Madam, the king with all his captains and his guards
Are forcing ope the doors. He threatens thousand deaths   115
To all that stop his entrance, and I believe
Your eunuchs will obey him.

ROXANA.

Then I must haste.   *Stabs her.*

STATIRA.   What, is the king so near?
And shall I die so tamely, thus defenseless?
O ye good gods! Will you not help my weakness?   120

ROXANA (*stabbing her*).

They are far off.

STATIRA.   Alas! They are indeed.

Enter Alexander, Cassander, Polyperchon, [Meleager,] *guards and attendants*.

ALEXANDER.

O harpy! Thou shalt reign the queen of devils.

ROXANA.

Do, strike! Behold, my bosom swells to meet thee;
'Tis full of thine, of veins that run ambition,
And I can brave whatever fate you bring.   125

ALEXANDER.

Call our physicians, haste! I'll give an empire
To save her. —O my soul, alas, Statira!
These wounds—O gods, are these my promised joys?

STATIRA.

My cruel love, my weeping Alexander,

Enter physicians.

Would I had died before you entered here,   130
For now I ask my heart a hundred questions.
What, must I lose my life, my lord, forever?

ALEXANDER.

    Ha! Villains, are they mortal? —What, retire!
    Raise your dashed spirits from the earth, and say,
    Say she shall live, and I will make you kings.　　135
    Give me this one, this poor, this only life,
    And I will pardon you for all the wounds
    Which your arts widen, all diseases, deaths
    Which your damned drugs throw through the ling'ring world.

ROXANA.

    Rend not your temper. See, a general silence　　140
    Confirms the bloody pleasure which I sought.
    She dies.—

ALEXANDER.　　And dar'st thou, monster, think to 'scape?

STATIRA.

    My life is on the wing, my love, my lord.
    Come to my arms and take the last adieu.
    Here let me lie, and languish out my soul.　　145

ALEXANDER.

    Answer me, father, wilt thou take her from me?
    What, is the black, sad hour at last arrived
    That I must never clasp her body more?
    Never more bask in her eyes' shine again,
    Nor view the loves that played in those dear beams,　　150
    And shot me with a thousand thousand smiles.

STATIRA.

    Farewell, my dear, my life, my most loved lord.
    I swear by Orosmades, 'tis more pleasure,
    More satisfaction, that I thus die yours,
    Than to have lived another's. Grant me one thing.　　155

ALEXANDER.

    All, all! But speak, that I may execute
    Before I follow thee.

STATIRA.　　　　Leave not the earth
    Before heav'n calls you. Spare Roxana's life;
    'Twas love of you that caused her give me death.
    And, O, sometimes amidst your revels think　　160
    Of your poor queen, and ere the cheerful bowl

134. your] *Q1, Q3;* you *Q2.*　　142. 'scape] *Q1;* escape *Q2–3.*

133. *are . . . mortal*] i.e., are her wounds fatal?
146. *father*] i.e., Jupiter.

Salute your lips, crown it with one rich tear,
And I am happy.   *Dies.*
ALEXANDER.   Close not thy eyes.
Things of import I have to speak before
Thou tak'st thy journey. Tell the gods I'm coming   165
To give 'em an account of life and death,
And many other hundred thousand policies
That much concern the government of heav'n.—
O, she is gone! The talking soul is mute!
She's hushed. No voice, no music now is heard!   170
The bower of beauty is more still than death;
The roses fade, and the melodious bird
That waked their sweets has left 'em now forever.
ROXANA.
'Tis certain now you never shall enjoy her;
Therefore Roxana may have leave to hope   175
You will at last be kind for all my sufferings,
My torments, racks, for this last dreadful murder,
Which furious love of thee did bring upon me.
ALEXANDER.
O thou vile creature! Bear thee from my sight,
And thank Statira that thou art alive;   180
Else thou hadst perished. Yes, I would ha' rent
With my just hands that rock, that marble heart;
I would have dived through seas of blood to find it,
To tear the cruel quarry from its center.
ROXANA.
O, take me to your arms and hide my blushes.   185
I love you, spite of all your cruelties.
There is so much divinity about you,
I tremble to approach; yet here's my hold,
Nor will I leave the sacred robe, for such
Is ev'rything that touches that blest body.   190
I'll kiss it as the relic of a god,
And love shall grasp it with these dying hands.
ALEXANDER.
O, that thou wert a man, that I might drive
Thee round the world, and scatter thy contagion,
As gods hurl mortal plagues when they are angry.   195
ROXANA.
Do, drive me, hew me into smallest pieces.

My dust shall be inspired with a new fondness;
Still the love-motes shall play before your eyes
Where'er you go, however you despise.

ALEXANDER.

Away, there's not a glance that flies from thee   200
But like a basilisk comes winged with death.

ROXANA.

O speak not such harsh words, my royal master,   *Kneels.*
Look not so dreadful on your kneeling servant;
But take, dear sir, O, take me into grace,
By the dear babe, the burden of my womb,   205
That weighs me down when I would follow faster.
My knees are weary and my force is spent.
O, do not frown, but clear that angry brow!
Your eyes will blast me, and your words are bolts
That strike me dead; the little wretch I bear   210
Leaps frighted at your wrath and dies within me.

ALEXANDER.

O, thou hast touched my soul so tenderly
That I will raise thee, though thy hands are ruin.
Rise, cruel woman, rise, and have a care.
O, do not hurt that unborn innocence,   215
For whose dear sake I now forgive thee all.
But haste, begone, fly, fly from these sad eyes,
Fly with thy pardon, lest I call it back;
Though I forgive thee, I must hate thee ever.

ROXANA.

I go, I fly forever from thy sight.   220
My mortal injuries have turned my mind,
And I could curse myself for being kind.
If there be any majesty above
That has revenge in store for perjured love,
Send heav'n the swiftest ruin on his head,   225
Strike the destroyer, lay the victor dead,
Kill the triumpher, and avenge my wrong   ⎫
In height of pomp while he is warm and young, ⎬
Bolted with thunder let him rush along.   ⎭
And when in the last pangs of life he lies,   230

202. S.D. *Kneels.*] *Q1; om. Q2–3.*

201. *basilisk*] cockatrice; see II.25 n.

  Grant I may stand to dart him with my eyes;
  Nay, after death,
  Pursue his spotted ghost, and shoot him as he flies.   *Exit.*

ALEXANDER.

  O my fair star! I shall be shortly with thee;
  For I already feel the sad effects   235
  Of those most fatal imprecations.
  What means this deadly dew upon my forehead?
  My heart, too, heaves.

CASSANDER (*aside*).   It will anon be still.
  The poison works.

POLYPERCHON (*aside*). I'll see the wished effect
  Ere I remove, and gorge me with revenge.   240

     Enter Perdiccas *and* Lysimachus.

PERDICCAS.

  I beg your majesty will pardon me,
  A fatal messenger. Great Sysigambis,
  Hearing Statira's death, is now no more.
  Her last words gave the princess to the brave
  Lysimachus; but that which most will strike you, 245
  Your dear Hephestion, having drank too largely
  At your last feast, is of a surfeit dead.

ALEXANDER.

  How, dead! Hephestion dead! Alas, the dear
  Unhappy youth! But he sleeps happy;
  I must wake forever. This object, this,   250
  This face of fatal beauty,
  Will stretch my lids with vast, eternal tears.—
  Who had the care of poor Hephestion's life?

LYSIMACHUS.

  Philarda, the Arabian artist.

ALEXANDER.

  Fly, Meleager, hang him on a cross: 255
  That for Hephestion.—
  But here lies my fate. Hephestion, Clytus,
  All my victories forever folded up.

242–243. A . . . more.] *Q 1–3 print* Great . . . death,/ Is . . . more.
as three lines: A . . . messenger;/

In this dear body my banners lost,
My standard's triumphs gone!   260
O, when shall I be mad? —Give order to
The army that they break their shields, swords, spears,
Pound their bright armor into dust away.
Is there not cause to put the world in mourning?
Tear all your robes. He dies that is not naked   265
Down to the waist, all like the sons of sorrow.
Burn all the spires that seem to kiss the sky;
Beat down the battlements of every city;
And for the monument of this loved creature,
Root up those bowers and pave 'em all with gold;   270
Draw dry the Ganges, make the Indies poor;
To build her tomb no shrines nor altars spare,
But strip the shining gods to make it rare.

Exit [with all but Cassander *and* Polyperchon].

CASSANDER.

Ha! Whither now? Follow him, Polyperchon.

Exit Polyperchon.

I find Cassander's plot grows full of death.   275
Murder is playing her great masterpiece,
And the sad sisters sweat, so fast I urge 'em.
O, how I hug myself for this revenge!
My fancy's great in mischief; for methinks
The night grows darker, and the lab'ring ghosts,   280
For fear that I should find new tortures out,
Run o'er the old with most prodigious swiftness.
I see the fatal fruit betwixt the teeth,
The sieve brimful, and the swift stone stand still.

259. banners] *Q1;* banner's *Q2–3.*   triumph's *Q2–3.*
260. standard's triumphs] *C3;* stan-   281. tortures] *Q1;* torments *Q2–3.*
dards   triumphs   *Q1;*   standard's

277. *sad sisters*] i.e., the three Fates.
279. *fancy*] imagination.
283–284.] Tantalus was punished with a raging thirst and surrounded by
water and branches of fruit which receded whenever he tried to reach them.
The fifty daughters of Danaus were condemned everlastingly to pour water
into a perforated jar. Sisyphus was obliged to push uphill a stone which
rolled back whenever it reached the summit. Cassander imagines that, in
their fear of him, the spirits of the damned actually accomplish the impossible tasks set them.

Enter Polyperchon.

What, does it work?

POLYPERCHON.   Speak softly.

CASSANDER.   Well?

POLYPERCHON.   It does.   285

I followed him, and saw him swiftly walk
Toward the palace, ofttimes looking back
With wat'ry eyes, and calling out, "Statira."
He stumbled at the gate and fell along;
Nor was he raised with ease by his attendants,   290
But seemed a greater load than ordinary,
As much more as the dead outweigh the living.

CASSANDER.

Said he nothing?

POLYPERCHON.   When they took him up,
He sighed, and entered with a strange, wild look,
Embraced the princes round, and said he must   295
Dispatch the business of the world in haste.

Enter Philip *and* Thessalus.

PHILIP.

Back, back! All scatter! With a dreadful shout
I heard him cry, "I am but a dead man."

THESSALUS.

The poison tears him with that height of horror
That I could pity him.   300

POLYPERCHON.

Peace! Where shall we meet?

CASSANDER.   In Saturn's field.
Methinks I see the frighted deities
Ramming more bolts in their big-bellied clouds,
And firing all the heav'ns to drown his noise.
Now we should laugh. But go, disperse yourselves,   305
While each soul here, that fills his noble vessel,
Swells with the murder, works with ruin o'er,
And from the dreadful deed this glory draws:
We killed the greatest man that ever was.   [*Exeunt.*]

301. field.] *Q 1–3;* field *M-J.*

306. *vessel*] formerly often used of the body as the receptacle of the soul.
307. *works . . . o'er*] i.e., rises over the brim (like fermenting liquor).

[V.ii]

The scene draws. Enter Alexander *and all his attendants*[, Lysimachus, Eumenes *and* Perdiccas].

ALEXANDER.

    Search there, nay probe me, search my wounded reins.
    Pull, draw it out.

LYSIMACHUS.   We have searched, but find no hurt.

ALEXANDER.

    O, I am shot. A forked, burning arrow
    Sticks cross my shoulders; the sad venom flies
    Like lightning through my flesh, my blood, my marrow.   5

LYSIMACHUS.

    This must be treason.

PERDICCAS.   Would I could but guess.

ALEXANDER.

    Ha! What a change of torments I endure!
    A bolt of ice runs hizzing through my bowels.
    'Tis sure the arm of death. Give me a chair.
    Cover me, for I freeze, my teeth chatter,   10
    And my knees knock together.

PERDICCAS.

    Heav'n bless the king!

ALEXANDER.   Ha! Who talks of heav'n?
    I am all hell, I burn, I burn again.
    The war grows wondrous hot. Hey for the Tigris.
    Bear me, Bucephalus, amongst the billows.   15
    O, 'tis a noble beast! I would not change him
    For the best horse the sun has in his stable.
    For they are hot, their mangers full of coals,
    Their manes are flakes of lightning, curls of fire,
    And their red tails like meteors whisk about.   20

LYSIMACHUS.

    Help, all. Eumenes, help. I cannot hold him.

ALEXANDER.

    Ha, ha, ha. I shall die with laughter.
    Parmenio, Clytus, dost thou see yon fellow?
    That ragged soldier, that poor tattered Greek?

---

14. *Tigris*] river dividing Mesopotamia from Assyria.
15. *Bucephalus*] Alexander's famous horse.

See how he puts to flight the gaudy Persians,   25
With nothing but a rusty helmet on, through which
The grizzly bristles of his pushing beard
Drive 'em like pikes. Ha, ha, ha.

PERDICCAS.

How wild he talks!

LYSIMACHUS.   Yet warring in his wildness.

ALEXANDER.

Sound, sound, keep your ranks close. Ay, now they come. 30
O, the brave din, the noble clank of arms!
Charge, charge apace, and let the phalanx move!
Darius comes. —Ha! Let me in. None dare
To cross my fury. —Philotas is unhorsed. —Ay, 'tis Darius,
I see, I know him by the sparkling plumes   35
And his gold chariot drawn by ten white horses.
But like a tempest thus I pour upon him.—
He bleeds. With that last blow I brought him down.
He tumbles. Take him, snatch the imperial crown.—
They fly, they fly. —Follow, follow. —*Victoria, Victoria,* 40
Victoria. —O, let me sleep.

PERDICCAS.

Let's raise him softly and bear him to his bed.

ALEXANDER.

Hold! The least motion gives me sudden death;
My vital spirits are quite parched, burnt up,
And all my smoky entrails turned to ashes.   45

LYSIMACHUS.

When you, the brightest star that ever shone,
Shall set, it must be night with us forever.

ALEXANDER.

Let me embrace you all before I die.
Weep not, my dear companions, the good gods
Shall send you in my stead a nobler prince,   50
One that shall lead you forth with matchless conduct.

LYSIMACHUS.

Break not our hearts with such unkind expressions.

PERDICCAS.

We will not part with you, nor change for Mars.

40–41.] Lee may have intended two regular alexandrines.
51. *conduct*] leadership.

ALEXANDER.

    Perdiccas, take this ring,
    And see me laid in the temple of   55
    Jupiter Ammon.

LYSIMACHUS.

    To whom does your dread majesty bequeath
    The empire of the world?

ALEXANDER.   To him that is most worthy.

PERDICCAS.

    When will you, sacred sir, that we should give
    To your great memory those divine honors   60
    Which such exalted virtue does deserve?

ALEXANDER.

    When you are all most happy, and in peace.
    Your hands.—   *Rises.*
              O father, if I have discharged
    The duty of a man to empire born;
    If by unwearied toil I have deserved   65
    The vast renown of thy adopted son,
    Accept this soul, which thou didst first inspire,
    And with this sigh, thus gives thee back again.   *Dies.*

LASIMACHUS.

    Eumenes, cover the fall'n majesty.
    If there be treason, let us find it out.   70
    Lysimachus stands forth to lead you on,
    And swears by those most honored, dear remains,
    He will not taste the joys which beauty brings
    Till we revenge the greatest, best of kings.   [*Exeunt.*]

FINIS

   54–57.] It is just conceivable that Lee may have intended two regular
lines: "Perdiccas . . . laid/ In . . . Ammon."

EPILOGUE

Whate'er they mean, yet ought they to be curst
Who this censorious age did polish first,
Who the best play for one poor error blame, ⎫
As priests against our ladies' arts declaim, ⎬
And for one patch both soul and body damn. ⎭   5
But what does more provoke the actors' rage
(For we must show the grievance of the stage)
Is that our women, who adorn each play,
Bred at our cost, become at length your prey.
While green and sour, like trees, we bear 'em all,   10
But when they're mellow, straight to you they fall.
You watch 'em bare and squab, and let 'em rest,
But with the first young down, you snatch the nest.
Pray leave these poaching tricks, if you are wise,
Ere we take out our letters of reprise.   15
For we have vowed to find a sort of toys
Known to black friars, a tribe of chopping boys.
If once they come, they'll quickly spoil your sport;
There's not one lady will receive your court,
But for the youth in petticoats run wild,   20
With, "O, the archest wag, the sweetest child."
The panting breasts, white hands and little feet
No more shall your palled thoughts with pleasure meet.

10. like] *Q2–3;* likes *Q1.*   22. breasts] *Q1;* breast *Q2–3.*
17. chopping] *Q3;* choopping *Q1;*   22. little feet] *Q1;* lilly-feet *Q2–3.*
chooping *Q2.*

---

5. *patch*] small, black, cosmetic patch (usually silk) worn on the face.
8–9.] Many actresses at this period left the stage to become kept mistresses.
12. *squab*] unfledged.
15. *letters of reprise*] letters of reprisal; "an official warrant authorizing an aggrieved subject to exact forcible reparation from the subjects of another state" (*OED*).
16. *sort*] probably in the obsolete sense of "company, band."
17. *Known . . . friars*] a reference to Blackfriars theater (dismantled 1655) which was earlier used by companies of boy actors and then by the King's Men with boys acting women's parts. Lee may also have intended an antipapist pun.
17. *chopping*] strapping.
21. *wag*] term of endearment for a mischievous boy or youth.

The woman in boys' clothes all boy shall be
And never raise your thoughts above the knee.   25
Well, if our women knew how false you are,
They would stay here and this new trouble spare.
Poor souls, they think all gospel, you relate,
Charmed with the noise of sett'ling an estate.
But when at last your appetites are full,   30
And the tired Cupid grows with action dull,
You'll find some trick to cut off the entail,
And send 'em back to us all worn and stale.
Perhaps they'll find our stage, while they have ranged,
To some vile, canting conventicle changed;   35
Where, for the sparks who once resorted there ⎫
With their curled wigs that scented all the air, ⎬
They'll see grave blockheads with short, greasy hair, ⎭
Green aprons, steeple-hats, and collar bands,
Dull, sniv'ling rogues that wring, not clap, their hands;   40
Where, for gay punks that drew the shining crowd,
And misses that in vizard laughed aloud,
They'll hear young sisters sigh, see matrons old
To their chopped cheeks their pickled kerchers hold,
Whose zeal, too, might persuade, in spite to you,   45
Our flying angels to augment their crew;

---

24. *woman . . . clothes*] Women disguised as boys figure in many plays of
the period.

29. *sett'ling an estate*] making a jointure, or estate settled on a wife in the
event of her husband's death.

32. *entail*] "the settlement of the succession of a landed estate, so that it
cannot be bequeathed at pleasure by any one possessor" (*OED*).

35. *canting*] using the hypocritical religious jargon and whining tone
associated with dissenters.

35. *conventicle*] meeting-house for dissenters.

38. *greasy*] Wigs were dusted with scented powder.

39. *Green aprons*] contemptuous term for lay preachers.

42. *vizard*] face mask; often worn by prostitutes.

43. *sisters*] female dissenters.

44. *chopped*] cracked, wrinkled.

44. *pickled*] in a "pickle."

44. *kerchers*] kerchiefs; cloths for covering the head, neck, shoulders, or
breasts.

46. *flying angels*] i.e., the departing actresses.

While Farringdon, their hero, struts about 'em,
And ne'er a damning critic dares to flout 'em.

---

47. *Farringdon*] William Farrington, a Presbyterian minister, who preached to large congregations in the old Theatre Royal in Vere Street after it was abandoned as an active playhouse in 1671: see A. G. Matthews, *Calamy Revised* (Oxford, 1934), p. 191.

Appendix

Chronology

Approximate years are indicated by *. Dates for plays are those on which they were first made public, either on stage or in print.

Political and Literary Events	*Life and Works of Nathaniel Lee*
1631	
Death of Donne.	
John Dryden born.	
1633	
Samuel Pepys born.	
1635	
Sir George Etherege born.*	
1640	
Aphra Behn born.*	
1641	
William Wycherley born.*	
1642	
First Civil War began (ended 1646).	
Theaters closed by Parliament.	
Thomas Shadwell born.*	
1648	
Second Civil War.	Born.*
1649	
Execution of Charles I.	
1650	
Jeremy Collier born.	
1651	
Hobbes' *Leviathan* published.	
1652	
First Dutch War began (ended 1654).	
Thomas Otway born.	
1656	
D'Avenant's *THE SIEGE OF RHODES* performed at Rutland House.	

1657
John Dennis born.

1658
Death of Oliver Cromwell.
D'Avenant's *THE CRUELTY OF THE SPANIARDS IN PERU* performed at the Cockpit.

Nominated to Charterhouse on May 20.

1660
Restoration of Charles II.
Theatrical patents granted to Thomas Killigrew and Sir William D'Avenant, authorizing them to form, respectively, the King's and the Duke of York's Companies.
Pepys began his diary.

1661
Cowley's *THE CUTTER OF COLEMAN STREET.*
D'Avenant's *THE SIEGE OF RHODES* (expanded to two parts).

1662
Charter granted to the Royal Society.

1663
Dryden's *THE WILD GALLANT.*
Tuke's *THE ADVENTURES OF FIVE HOURS.*

1664
Sir John Vanbrugh born.
Dryden's *THE RIVAL LADIES.*
Dryden and Howard's *THE INDIAN QUEEN.*
Etherege's *THE COMICAL REVENGE.*

1665
Second Dutch War began (ended 1667).
Great Plague.
Dryden's *THE INDIAN EMPEROR.*
Orrery's *MUSTAPHA.*

Entered Trinity College, Cambridge, on July 7.

1666
Fire of London.
Death of James Shirley.

1667
Jonathan Swift born.

Milton's *Paradise Lost* published.
Sprat's *The History of the Royal Society* published.
Dryden's *SECRET LOVE.*

1668
Death of D'Avenant.
Dryden made Poet Laureate.
Dryden's *An Essay of Dramatic Poesy* published.
Shadwell's *THE SULLEN LOVERS.*

1669
Pepys terminated his diary.   B.A. from Cambridge.
Susanna Centlivre born.

1670
William Congreve born.
Dryden's *THE CONQUEST OF GRANADA*, Part I.

1671
Dorset Garden Theatre (Duke's Company) opened.
Colley Cibber born.
Milton's *Paradise Regained* and *Samson Agonistes* published.
Dryden's *THE CONQUEST OF GRANADA*, Part II.
THE REHEARSAL, by the Duke of Buckingham and others.
Wycherley's *LOVE IN A WOOD.*

1672
Third Dutch War began (ended   Actor in the Duke's Company.
1674).
Joseph Addison born.
Richard Steele born.
Dryden's *MARRIAGE A LA MODE.*

1674
New Drury Lane Theatre (King's   *THE TRAGEDY OF NERO, EM-*
Company) opened.   *PEROR OF ROME* produced in
Death of Milton.   May at Drury Lane.
Nicholas Rowe born.
Thomas Rymer's *Reflections on Aristotle's Treatise of Poesy* (translation of Rapin) published.

1675
Dryden's *AURENG-ZEBE.*   *SOPHONISBA, OR HANNIBAL'S*
Wycherley's *THE COUNTRY*   *OVERTHROW* produced in April
*WIFE.**   in Drury Lane.

−105−

1676

Etherege's *THE MAN OF MODE.*
Otway's *DON CARLOS.*
Shadwell's *THE VIRTUOSO.*
Wycherley's *THE PLAIN DEALER.*

GLORIANA, OR THE COURT OF AUGUSTUS CAESAR produced in January at Drury Lane.

1677

Aphra Behn's *THE ROVER.*
Rymer's *Tragedies of the Last Age Considered* published.
Dryden's *ALL FOR LOVE.*

THE RIVAL QUEENS, OR THE DEATH OF ALEXANDER THE GREAT produced in March at Drury Lane.

1678

Popish Plot.
George Farquhar born.
Bunyan's *Pilgrim's Progress* (Part I) published.

MITHRIDATES, KING OF PONTUS produced in March* at Drury Lane; *OEDIPUS* (in collaboration with Dryden) produced in November* at Dorset Garden.

1679

Exclusion Bill introduced.
Death of Thomas Hobbes.
Death of Roger Boyle, Earl of Orrery.
Charles Johnson born.

CAESAR BORGIA: THE SON OF POPE ALEXANDER THE SIXTH produced in September* at Dorset Garden.

1680

Death of Samuel Butler.
Death of John Wilmot, Earl of Rochester.
Dryden's *THE SPANISH FRIAR.*
Otway's *THE ORPHAN.*

THE PRINCESS OF CLEVE produced* at Dorset Garden; *THEODOSIUS; OR, THE FORCE OF LOVE* produced in September* at Dorset Garden; *LUCIUS JUNIUS BRUTUS* produced in December at Dorset Garden.

1681

Charles II dissolved Parliament at Oxford.
Dryden's *Absalom and Achitophel* published.
Tate's adaptation of *KING LEAR.*

1682

The King's and the Duke of York's Companies merged into the United Company.
Dryden's *The Medal, MacFlecknoe,* and *Religio Laici* published.
Otway's *VENICE PRESERVED.*

THE DUKE OF GUISE (in collaboration with Dryden) produced in November at Drury Lane.

1683

Rye House Plot.
Death of Thomas Killigrew.

CONSTANTINE THE GREAT produced* at Drury Lane.

Crowne's *CITY POLITIQUES*.
1684

Committed to Bedlam Hospital on November 11.

1685
Death of Charles II; accession of James II.
Revocation of the Edict of Nantes.
The Duke of Monmouth's Rebellion.
Death of Otway.
John Gay born.
Crowne's *SIR COURTLY NICE*.
Dryden's *ALBION AND ALBANIUS*.

1687
Death of the Duke of Buckingham.
Dryden's *The Hind and the Panther* published.
Newton's *Principia* published.

1688
The Revolution.
Alexander Pope born.
Shadwell's *THE SQUIRE OF ALSATIA*.

Released from Bedlam on April 11.

1689
The War of the League of Augsburg began (ended 1697).
Toleration Act.
Death of Aphra Behn.
Shadwell made Poet Laureate.
Dryden's *DON SEBASTIAN*.
Shadwell's *BURY FAIR*.

THE MASSACRE OF PARIS (written about 1678 and suppressed by the authorities) produced November 7 at Drury Lane.

1690
Battle of the Boyne.
Locke's *Two Treatises of Government* and *An Essay Concerning Human Understanding* published.

1691
Death of Etherege.*
Langbaine's *An Account of the English Dramatic Poets* published.

1692
Death of Shadwell.
Tate made Poet Laureate.

Death in May.

1693
George Lillo born.*

Rymer's *A Short View of Tragedy* published.
Congreve's *THE OLD BACHELOR*.

1694
Death of Queen Mary.
Southerne's *THE FATAL MAR-RIAGE*.

1695
Group of actors led by Thomas Betterton left Drury Lane and established a new company at Lincoln's Inn Fields.
Congreve's *LOVE FOR LOVE*.
Southerne's *OROONOKO*.

1696
Cibber's *LOVE'S LAST SHIFT*.
Vanbrugh's *THE RELAPSE*.

1697
Treaty of Ryswick ended the War of the League of Augsburg.
Charles Macklin born.
Congreve's *THE MOURNING BRIDE*.
Vanbrugh's *THE PROVOKED WIFE*.

1698
Collier controversy started with the publication of *A Short View of the Immorality and Profaneness of the English Stage*.

1699
Farquhar's *THE CONSTANT COUPLE*.

1700
Death of Dryden.
Blackmore's *Satire against Wit* published.
Congreve's *THE WAY OF THE WORLD*.

1701
Act of Settlement.
War of the Spanish Succession began (ended 1713).
Death of James II.
Rowe's *TAMERLANE*.
Steele's *THE FUNERAL*.

1702

Death of William III; accession of Anne.

The Daily Courant began publication.

Cibber's *SHE WOULD AND SHE WOULD NOT.*

1703

Death of Samuel Pepys.

Rowe's *THE FAIR PENITENT.*

1704

Capture of Gibraltar; Battle of Blenheim.

Defoe's *The Review* began publication (1704–1713).

Swift's *A Tale of a Tub* and *The Battle of the Books* published.

Cibber's *THE CARELESS HUSBAND.*

1705

Haymarket Theatre opened.

Steele's *THE TENDER HUSBAND.*

1706

Battle of Ramillies.

Farquhar's *THE RECRUITING OFFICER.*

1707

Union of Scotland and England.

Death of Farquhar.

Henry Fielding born.

Farquhar's *THE BEAUX' STRATAGEM.*

1708

Downes' *Roscius Anglicanus* published.

1709

Samuel Johnson born.

Rowe's edition of Shakespeare published.

The Tatler began publication (1709–1711).

Centilivre's *THE BUSY BODY.*

1711

Shaftesbury's *Characteristics* published.

The Spectator began publication (1711–1712).

Pope's *An Essay on Criticism* published.

1713
Treaty of Utrecht ended the War of the Spanish Succession.
Addison's *CATO*.

1714
Death of Anne; accession of George I.
Steele became Governor of Drury Lane.
John Rich assumed management of Lincoln's Inn Fields.
Centlivre's *THE WONDER: A WOMAN KEEPS A SECRET*.
Rowe's *JANE SHORE*.

1715
Jacobite Rebellion.
Death of Tate.
Rowe made Poet Laureate.
Death of Wycherley.

1716
Addison's *THE DRUMMER*.

1717
David Garrick born.
Cibber's *THE NON-JUROR*.
Gay, Pope, and Arbuthnot's *THREE HOURS AFTER MARRIAGE*.

1718
Death of Rowe.
Centlivre's *A BOLD STROKE FOR A WIFE*.

1719
Death of Addison.
Defoe's *Robinson Crusoe* published.
Young's *BUSIRIS, KING OF EGYPT*.

1720
South Sea Bubble.
Samuel Foote born.
Steele suspended from the Governorship of Drury Lane (restored 1721).
Little Theatre in the Haymarket opened.

Steele's *The Theatre* (periodical) published.
Hughes' *THE SIEGE OF DAMAS-CUS*.

1721
Walpole became first Minister.

1722
Steele's *THE CONSCIOUS LOVERS*.

1723
Death of Susanna Centlivre.
Death of D'Urfey.

1725
Pope's edition of Shakespeare published.

1726
Death of Jeremy Collier.
Death of Vanbrugh.
Law's *Unlawfulness of State Entertainments* published.
Swift's *Gulliver's Travels* published.

1727
Death of George I; accession of George II.
Death of Sir Isaac Newton.
Arthur Murphy born.

1728
Pope's *The Dunciad* (first version) published.
Cibber's *THE PROVOKED HUS-BAND* (expansion of Vanbrugh's fragment *A JOURNEY TO LON-DON*).
Gay's *THE BEGGAR'S OPERA*.

1729
Goodman's Fields Theatre opened.
Death of Congreve.
Death of Steele.
Edmund Burke born.

1730
Cibber made Poet Laureate.
Oliver Goldsmith born.
Thomson's *The Seasons* published.
Fielding's *THE AUTHOR'S FARCE*.

Fielding's *TOM THUMB* (revised as *THE TRAGEDY OF TRAG-EDIES*, 1731).

1731
Death of Defoe.
Fielding's *THE GRUB-STREET OPERA*.
Lillo's *THE LONDON MER-CHANT*.

1732
Covent Garden Theatre opened.
Death of Gay.
George Colman the elder born.
Fielding's *THE COVENT GAR-DEN TRAGEDY*.
Fielding's *THE MODERN HUS-BAND*.
Charles Johnson's *CAELIA*.

1733
Pope's *An Essay on Man* (Epistles I–III) published (Epistle IV, 1734).

1734
Death of Dennis.
The Prompter began publication (1734–1736).
Theobald's edition of Shakespeare published.
Fielding's *DON QUIXOTE IN ENGLAND*.

1736
Fielding led the "Great Mogul's Company of Comedians" at the Little Theatre in the Haymarket (1736–1737).
Fielding's *PASQUIN*.
Lillo's *FATAL CURIOSITY*.

1737
The Stage Licensing Act.
Dodsley's *THE KING AND THE MILLER OF MANSFIELD*.
Fielding's *THE HISTORICAL REGISTER FOR 1736*.